UNDERSTANDING
SHERMAN ALEXIE

Understanding Contemporary American Literature
Matthew J. Bruccoli, Series Editor

Volumes on

Edward Albee • Sherman Alexie • Nicholson Baker • John Barth
Donald Barthelme • The Beats • The Black Mountain Poets
Robert Bly • Raymond Carver • Fred Chappell
Chicano Literature • Contemporary American Drama
Contemporary American Horror Fiction
Contemporary American Literary Theory
Contemporary American Science Fiction
Contemporary Chicana Literature • Robert Coover
James Dickey • E. L. Doctorow • John Gardner • George Garrett
John Hawkes • Joseph Heller • Lillian Hellman • John Irving
Randall Jarrell • Charles Johnson • William Kennedy
Jack Kerouac Ursula K. Le Guin • Denise Levertov
Bernard Malamud • Bobbie Ann Mason • Jill McCorkle
Carson McCullers • W. S. Merwin • Arthur Miller
Toni Morrison's Fiction • Vladimir Nabokov • Gloria Naylor
Joyce Carol Oates • Tim O'Brien • Flannery O'Connor
Cynthia Ozick • Walker Percy • Katherine Anne Porter
Richard Powers • Reynolds Price • Annie Proulx • Thomas Pynchon
Theodore Roethke • Philip Roth • May Sarton • Hubert Selby, Jr.
Mary Lee Settle • Neil Simon • Isaac Bashevis Singer • Jane Smiley
Gary Snyder • William Stafford • Anne Tyler • Kurt Vonnegut
David Foster Wallace • Robert Penn Warren • James Welch
Eudora Welty • Tennessee Williams • August Wilson

UNDERSTANDING
SHERMAN
ALEXIE

Daniel Grassian

University of South Carolina Press

© 2005 University of South Carolina

Published in Columbia, South Carolina,
by the University of South Carolina Press

Manufactured in the United States of America

09 08 07 06 05   5 4 3 2 1

            Library of Congress Cataloging-in-Publication Data
Grassian, Daniel, 1974–
   Understanding Sherman Alexie / Daniel Grassian.
       p. cm. — (Understanding contemporary American literature)
   Includes bibliographical references and index.
   ISBN 1-57003-571-7 (cloth : alk. paper)
   1. Alexie, Sherman, 1966– —Criticism and interpretation. 2. Indians in
literature. I. Title. II. Series.
   PS3551.L35774Z67 2005
   818'.5409—dc22

                                                              2004019058

Contents

Series Editor's Preface / vii

Chapter 1
   Understanding Sherman Alexie / 1

Chapter 2
   The Business of Fancydancing and *Old Shirts and New Skins* / 15

Chapter 3
   First Indian on the Moon and *The Lone Ranger and Tonto Fistfight in Heaven* / 40

Chapter 4
   Reservation Blues / 78

Chapter 5
   Indian Killer / 104

Chapter 6
   The Summer of Black Widows and *One Stick Song* / 127

Chapter 7
   The Toughest Indian in the World / 151

Chapter 8
   Ten Little Indians / 173

Notes / 193
Bibliography / 203
Index / 207

Series Editor's Preface

The volumes of *Understanding Contemporary American Literature* have been planned as guides or companions for students as well as good nonacademic readers. The editor and publisher perceive a need for these volumes because much of the influential contemporary literature makes special demands. Uninitiated readers encounter difficulty in approaching works that depart from the traditional forms and techniques of prose and poetry. Literature relies on conventions, but the conventions keep evolving; new writers form their own conventions—which in time may become familiar. Put simply, *UCAL* provides instruction in how to read certain contemporary writers—identifying and explicating their material, themes, use of language, point of view, structures, symbolism, and responses to experience.

The word *understanding* in the titles was deliberately chosen. Many willing readers lack an adequate understanding of how contemporary literature works; that is, what the author is attempting to express and the means by which it is conveyed. Although the criticism and analysis in the series have been aimed at a level of general accessibility, these introductory volumes are meant to be applied in conjunction with the works they cover. They do not provide a substitute for the works and authors they introduce, but rather prepare the reader for more profitable literary experiences.

M. J. B.

UNDERSTANDING
SHERMAN ALEXIE

CHAPTER 1

Understanding Sherman Alexie

Sherman Alexie was born on October 7, 1966, in the town of Wellpinit on the 156,000-acre Spokane Indian Reservation in eastern Washington state, a town of approximately one thousand people. Alexie describes the Spokanes as "a Salmon people. Our religions, our cultures, our dancing, our singing—had everything to do with the salmon. We were devastated by the Grand Coulee Dam. It took 7,000 miles of salmon spawning beds from the interior Indians in Washington, Idaho and Montana."[1] He also credits the establishment of casinos on the reservation for producing an economic turnaround: "On my reservation, there was about 90 percent unemployment before bingo halls and casinos; now it's about 10 percent."[2]

Alexie's father, Sherman Sr., a Coeur d'Alene Indian who occasionally worked as a logger and truck driver, was a heavy drinker who would often abandon the family for days at a time. Alexie's mother, of Spokane Indian descent, scraped together money by sewing and working as a clerk to support Alexie and his five siblings. Alexie was born with hydrocephalus, "a life-threatening condition marked by an abnormally large amount of cerebrospinal fluid in the cranial cavity."[3] At six months, he underwent dangerous surgery to correct the hydrocephalus. The doctors did not expect him to survive or, if so, only with severe mental handicaps, but Alexie proved them wrong, although throughout much of his childhood he suffered some severe side effects from the surgery, including an enlarged skull, seizures, and uncontrollable bed-wetting.

As a result of his physical abnormalities, Alexie was frequently mocked and ostracized by the other children, some of whom called him "The Globe" because of his large head. Alexie found refuge in books and in school, reading every book in the Wellpinit School library by the time he was twelve. Furthermore, he quickly learned the value of humor both as a means of deflecting the abuse from other children and also as a means of personal empowerment. Alexie explains his rationale: "You can't run as fast or throw or a punch if you're laughing."[4] Furthermore, he would later claim, "Humor is self-defense on the rez. You make people laugh and you disarm them. You sort of sneak up on them. You can say controversial or rowdy things and they'll listen or laugh."[5]

Educated mainly in mainstream, predominantly white schools, Alexie has only a rudimentary knowledge of the Spokane language, as his mother believed that he would succeed with proficiency in English and with a mainstream American education. After attending tribal school through eighth grade, Alexie transferred to an all-white high school in Reardon, Washington. While he felt somewhat isolated there as the only Indian student, Alexie adjusted to the new environment well, "becoming a star player on the school's basketball team, as well as the team captain, class president, and a member of the championship debate team."[6]

After graduating from high school with honors, Alexie began college at Gonzaga University, a Jesuit school in Spokane, in 1985. The privileged, predominantly white Gonzaga students did not impress Alexie much, nor did the elitist, social environment. Over time, Alexie's studies deteriorated due to heavy drinking and, after two years, he dropped out of school. Subsequently, he moved to Seattle, where he worked as a busboy. On his twenty-first birthday, Alexie was robbed at knifepoint and had an epiphany, deciding to change the direction of his life by going back to school, this time at Washington State University.

Although Alexie initially planned on medicine as a career, he found that his frequent fainting in anatomy class was a dubious sign of his possible future as a doctor. Without serious premeditation, he signed up for a poetry-writing workshop with Alex Kuo. In this class, Alexie read his first volume of Native American poetry, *Songs from This Earth on Turtle's Back*. The anthology was eye-opening for Alexie, who recalls, "I opened it up and—oh my gosh—I saw my life in poems and stories for the very first time."[7] Inspired by the poems in the collection, Alexie started writing his own.[8] His instructor, Alex Kuo, was greatly impressed by Alexie's work and encouraged him to pursue writing as a career.

In 1991 Alexie finished his studies and received a bachelor's degree in American Studies from Washington State. After graduation, he briefly worked as an administrator at a Spokane high school while continuing to write and publish poetry. One of the publishers that frequently published Alexie's poems, Hanging Loose Press, agreed to publish a collection of his poetry in 1992 as *The Business of Fancydancing*. Alexie chose the day on which he learned of its acceptance for publication to stop drinking for good.[9] Also, he received an enormous professional boost when James Kincaid from the *New York Times* gave his book effusive praise, calling Alexie "one of the major lyric voices of our time."[10] Alexie quickly followed *The Business of Fancydancing* with a small poetry chapbook, *I Would Steal Horses,* published by Slipstream Press in the same year, and another book of poetry, *First Indian on the Moon* (1993).

After hearing of and/or reading the glowing reviews of his poetry, publishers and literary agents asked Alexie for a fiction manuscript. He had a few stories on reserve, but ended up writing over half of *The Lone Ranger and Tonto Fistfight in Heaven* "in three months, in between the review and when I submitted the book to agents."[11] *The Lone Ranger and Tonto Fistfight in Heaven* was a finalist for the PEN/Hemingway Award. His follow-up work, the novel *Reservation Blues,* won the Before Columbus Foundation's American Book Award. After *Reservation Blues* came the novel *Indian Killer* (1996) and a book of poetry, *The Summer of Black Widows* (1996).

In that same year (1996), Alexie was honored by *Granta* magazine as one of the twenty best American novelists under the age of forty. Comically self-deprecating, Alexie downplays the honor, explaining, "It's because they needed a brown guy."[12] After the publication of *Indian Killer* and *The Summer of Black Widows,* Alexie changed directions, writing a screenplay loosely based on a few stories in *The Lone Ranger and Tonto Fistfight in Heaven,* most specifically, "This Is What It Means to Say, Phoenix, Arizona." This screenplay became the feature film *Smoke Signals* (1998), directed by Chris Eyre, a Native American filmmaker. Whereas previous movies (such as *Powwow Highway* and *Navajo Blues*) had focused upon Native Americans and many more had Native Americans playing significant roles (such as *Dances with Wolves*), *Smoke Signals* became, as Alexie explains, "the first feature film written, directed and co-produced by Indians ever to receive a major distribution deal."[13] The filmmaking experience took some adjustment for Alexie. "In writing books," he explains, "I am the Fidel Castro of my world. I determine everything. In the filmmaking project, I'm more like the senator from Wyoming. So getting used to that took some doing."[14] Still, the end product was a critical success. *Smoke Signals* won the Audience Award at the Sundance Film Festival in 1998; in addition, it was nominated for the Grand Jury Prize.

In recent years Alexie has returned to fiction and poetry with *One Stick Song* (2000), *The Toughest Indian in the World* (2001), and *Ten Little Indians* (2003). He also wrote, produced, and directed the film *The Business of Fancydancing* (2002), which concerns a trip home to a reservation by a gay Indian poet and his subsequent reevaluation of his childhood and his current identity. Alexie has also perfected his stage persona in poetry readings, becoming an oratorical success, winning the Taos Poetry Circus World Heavyweight Championship three years in a row (2000–2002).

Currently, Alexie lives in Seattle with his wife, Diane, and his two young sons. In an interview conducted in early 2003, Alexie explains how he has grown less attached to ethnic identity, culture, and traditions, disavowing his former claim that "Indians can reside in the city but never live there."[15] He explains:

I was much more fundamental then [in his earlier writing]. What changed me was September 11th [2001]: I am now desperately trying to let go of the idea of being right, the idea of making decisions based on imaginary tribes. The terrorists were flying planes into the buildings because they thought they were right and they had special knowledge, and we continue to react. And we will be going to war in Iraq soon because we think we have special knowledge—and we don't. We are making these decisions not based on any moral or ethical choice, but simply on the basis of power and money and ancient traditions that are full of shit, so I am increasingly suspicious of the word "tradition," whether in political or literary terms.[16]

In the near future, Alexie plans to publish a collection of poetry and a biography of Jimi Hendrix. He is also working on a memoir tracing his family history from his grandfather who died in the Second World War to his own children.

Much of Alexie's fiction and poetry takes place on the Spokane Indian Reservation where he was born and raised, and he uses recurring characters like the isolated storyteller, Thomas Builds-the-Fire, and the violent and troubled bully, Victor. In that sense, he is like William Faulkner, focusing upon a small geographical locale to explore larger issues. At the same time, Alexie is more of an autobiographical writer than Faulkner is, for unlike the invented Yoknapatawpha County, Alexie's Spokane reservation is an actual place where he finds a virtually inexhaustible literary wellspring for his writing. As Alexie explains, "Every theme, every story, every tragedy that exists in literature takes place in my little community. Hamlet takes place on my reservation daily. King Lear takes place on my reservation daily. It's a powerful place. I'm never going to run out of stories."[17] Furthermore, Alexie explains that one of his primary goals is to reach Indian children on the reservation, whom he believes to be mainly influenced by white-dominated popular culture. Toward that end, Alexie often uses references to television shows, movies, and music as a means to capture their attention and to speak in their language.[18] "It's the cultural currency," he explains. "Superman means something different to me than it does to a white guy from Ames, Iowa, or New York City or L.A. It's a way for us to sit at the same table. I use pop culture like most poets use Latin."[19] Specifically, Alexie describes television as the contemporary Gutenberg press, maintaining that "TV is the only thing that keeps us vaguely in democracy even if it's in the hands of the corporate culture."[20]

Alexie considers himself first and foremost a poet and short-story writer, then a novelist, screenwriter, and filmmaker. "These two things [poetry and short stories] are very natural," according to Alexie. "It's like breathing for me. I really have to struggle with novels. If I never had to write another novel again, I'd be happy. I like the contained world."[21] Working in the motion-picture industry affected Alexie's literary perspective, making him worry about the accessibility of his writing and its potential for film adaptation. Consequently, after making *Smoke Signals,* he decided only to make movies "in the same way that I write books: all by myself, with all of my inaccessible bullshit, all of my good and bad writing, and most of the soul I have left intact. I'm going to make very cheap movies on video, and manufacture and distribute the videos all by myself, free from as many corporate influences as possible."[22] To a large extent, this is what he did with his film *The Business of Fancydancing.*

Alexie's independent, even rebellious spirit is somewhat at odds with his use of ethnic categories. For the most part, he does not seek to tear down or question ethnic boundaries. For him, being Indian is the primary determinant of his identity and defines his writing: "If I write it, it's an Indian novel. If I wrote about Martians, it would be an Indian novel. If I wrote about the Amish, it would be an Indian novel. That's who I am."[23] He criticizes stereotypes of Indians as nature-loving noble savages and implicates what he calls "the corn-pollen, four directions, eagle-feathered school of Native literature."[24] "You throw in a couple of birds and four directions and corn pollen," Alexie explains, "and it's Native American literature, when it has nothing to do with the day-to-day lives of Indians. I want my literature to concern the daily lives of Indians."[25] Another of Alexie's purposes is to rewrite dominant American history, which barely acknowledges the violent colonization and subsequent massacres of Indians by European settlers, because, as Alexie suggests, to do so would severely damage American national identity and pride. "If people start dealing with Indian culture and Indian peoples truthfully in this country," he argues, "we're going to have to start dealing with the genocide that happened here. In order to start dealing truthfully with our cultures, they have to start dealing truthfully with that great sin, the original sin of this country, and that's not going to happen."[26]

It is important to recognize that Indians are not only indigenous to North America and a colonized people,[27] but they have been stereotyped and categorized by Europeans from their first settlements in the early seventeenth century. As Andrew Macdonald explains, "Since the first encounters of pre-colonial times, Europeans have shaped, changed, and distorted the indigenous people to serve white people's needs. The very word 'Indian' is a conflation of hundreds of tribes, languages, and cultures into one emblematic figure: the Other, the Alien, the generalized Non-European."[28] While Natives were first codified as savages by European settlers, who claimed land in the name of Manifest Destiny, over time they tended to think of Natives more as noble savages. "Europeans," William Bevis explains,

> have long assumed a serious split between man and nature, and after 1800, they have often preferred nature to man's works. Lacking respect for their own civilization, when

European whites have imagined a beatific union of "man and nature" they have assumed that the union would look not "human" but "natural"; therefore, they perceived the Indians as living in a "primitive" union of man and nature that was an antithesis of civilization.[29]

This conception of Native Americans as archetypal ecological figures continues to this day. With the development and subsequent spread of "New Age" interests in recent years, an increasing number of non-Natives have sought to appropriate Native ideas. Thereby, a kind of cultural colonialism has developed. Indeed, Jace Weaver and other Indian scholars insist that Natives are still colonized and oppressed by the white majority.[30]

In reality, life on the reservation is far from idyllic. It has been estimated that alcohol and drugs are responsible for more than half of the deaths on reservations.[31] While contemporary Indians do receive government-provided benefits if they have registered as a member of one of the 317 federally recognized tribes, those benefits hardly offset the bleak economic conditions of the reservation. As Jace Weaver explains:

> The average yearly income is half the poverty level, and over half of all Natives are unemployed. On some reservations, unemployment runs as high as 85–90 percent. Health statistics chronically rank Natives at or near the bottom. Male life expectancy is forty-four years, and female is forty-seven. . . . The worst part is that these statistics have not changed in thirty years. Substance abuse, suicide, crime, and violence are major problems among both urban and reservation populations.[32]

Furthermore, Indians are in danger of being subsumed by the white majority as "almost 60 percent of all American Indians are married to non-Indians." Only one-quarter of Natives speak a tribal language, and one-third have no tribal affiliation.[33]

Despite these seemingly bleak statistics, Indians have maintained rich oral traditions over the years. Still, European settlers were not aware of or concerned with Indian culture when they settled the country, and consistently, in colonial through nineteenth-century American literature, from Mary Rowlandson to Nathaniel Hawthorne and Mark Twain, Indians often appeared as uncivilized, demonic figures or, at best—in the work of James Fenimore Cooper—as noble savages.

Yet the twentieth century brought significant changes to the conceptions of Natives by Europeans. "The Great Depression," Norma Wilson explains,

> initiated an unprecedented interest in Native American culture and literature, as readers looked for enduring philosophies and lifestyles more in harmony with the land. The Civil Rights Movement inspired America's indigenous peoples, and by the late 1960s they had begun reasserting their sovereignty rights and producing a significant body of literature.[34]

It is generally thought that a Native American literary renaissance began in the late 1960s, with the publication of N. Scott Momaday's Pulitzer Prize–winning novel *House Made of Dawn* (1968), an account of a tortured war veteran, Abel, who is caught between the reservation and urban worlds. Momaday was quickly followed by critically acclaimed writers like James Welch, Leslie Marmon Silko, Gerald Vizenor, and Louise Erdrich.

There are some general differences between Native American fiction and mainstream European or American fiction. William Bevis claims that such canonical Western novels as *Moby-Dick, The Portrait of a Lady, The Adventures of Huckleberry*

Finn, and *The Great Gatsby* contain plots based upon leaving, escape, or discovery, in which "the individual advances, sometimes at all costs, with little or no regard for family, society, past, or place. The individual is the ultimate reality, hence individual consciousness is the medium, repository, and arbiter of knowledge."[35] In contrast to the typical Western plot, Bevis argues that in a typical Native American work, the protagonist "recoils from a white world in which the mobile Indian individual finds no meaning and as if by instinct, comes home. . . . This 'homing' cannot be judged by white standards of individuality; it must be read in the tribal context."[36]

Many of today's most successful Indian writers, including Alexie, find themselves caught between mainstream American life and reservation life. As James Ruppert explains, "Native American writers write for two audiences—non-Native and Native American—or in many cases three audiences—a local, a pan-tribal one and a non-Native contemporary American one. The attempt to satisfy those audiences generates the peculiar construct of their art."[37] Alexie, a member of "Generation X" and younger than his precursors Momaday, Welch, and Silko, faces a greater challenge: how to write about Indians in a predominantly televisual country.

One way that Alexie and many other Indian writers disrupt colonial influences is by playing the role of a trickster, an important figure in many Native cultures. While the role of the trickster varies from tribe to tribe, he generally "has a familiar set of characteristics: he plays tricks and is the victim of tricks; he is amoral and has strong appetites, particularly for food and sex; he is footloose, irresponsible and callous, but somehow always sympathetic if not lovable."[38] Gerald Vizenor calls the trickster an "androgynous, comic healer and liberator in literature,"[39] while Jace Weaver claims that Indian writers adopt the role of the trickster by adopting "a multiplicity of styles and forms to suit their purposes."[40]

Most contemporary American indigenous authors began by writing poetry.[41] Some have compared Native American poetry to English romantic poetry,[42] although that is a narrow generalization. Similar to early African American communities, "America's indigenous nations created songs to accompany every aspect of their lives—healing, hunting, planting, grinding corn, making poetry, dying, loving, making war."[43] Indian poetry is primarily oral, de-emphasizes rhyme, uses humor, and often focuses on the tribe and environment and upon the sacred and mystical. That the number of Native American poets has dramatically increased since the 1960s shows that more Indians have become interested in writing poetry and, presumably, that their audience has grown as well.

There are some general distinctions that can be made between Native American and Western or mainstream American perspectives. Traditionally, most Indian cultures believe in the sanctity of words, which, in the form of poems or stories, are thought to possess a life and power independent of the narrator. In "The Absence of the Sacred: The Failure of Technology and the Survival of the Indian Nations," Jerry Mander characterizes American society as hierarchical, materialistic, patriarchal, and ecologically unsound. In contrast, he views Indian cultures as nature-oriented, nonhierarchical, matriarchal, and spiritual. Vine Deloria Jr., a preeminent Native essayist, argues that the landscape plays a crucial role in Native American religion, identity, and, by consequence, literature. Their spatial organization, he argues, lies in marked contrast to the more temporal organization of Westerners. Echoing Deloria, Raymond Fogelson writes:

"The idea that land was property that could be exclusively possessed, expropriated, or alienated was foreign to native North America."[44] Furthermore, it has been argued that Native Americans typically have a more cyclical view of time and life rather than a more linear view.[45] Also, a crucial hallmark of Native culture is thought to be the "relationship of human beings to all other forms of existence in a vast web of cosmic interrelationship in which humans stand at the bottom or on the periphery."[46] While Native tribes tend to believe in a creator or creators, they rarely think of a singular deity with whom they could communicate, as do many Christians. For others, such as Cherokee writer Thomas King, community is the central feature of Native culture.[47] Indeed, Jace Weaver argues that Native American literature is most defined by "communitism," a "combination of community and activism."[48] While some writers like King believe that the conversion of Indians to Western religions has led to a deterioration of Native culture, community, and beliefs, Alexie is more ambivalent about the influence of Western religions upon Indians. While Alexie tends to criticize the deleterious influence of Catholicism and Christianity upon Native Americans, he considers the Jesuits more praiseworthy. "I love Jesuits," he explains. "They are the rock 'n' roll stars of the Catholic church. I love their mysticism, their social and economic politics. I love their poetic streak and their rebelliousness." Alexie admits, "I still am heavily Catholic- and Christian-influenced."[49]

In recent years, with the New Age movement, there has been an increase in interest in virtually all things deemed to be Native American or created by Natives. "Today," as Andrew Macdonald proposes,

mainstream America's sense of a lost past, an unrealized potential, and a life more in tune with the rhythms of the

Earth leads some to look back to pre-Columbian America and the Indians of that period as a lost utopia, a better world than the one we have created, or to see in the past the seeds of destruction that have swept away so many nations and cultures, and will sweep away so many more in the future.[50]

Alexie and many other Native authors regard the New Age movement with suspicion, viewing it as a misguided attempt on the part of white people to usurp Native culture largely for their own selfish purposes. Along similar lines, Alexie refuses to submit to mainstream standards for a watered-down, romanticized version of Native American literature. He is determined to remain fiercely independent, without catering to any specific audience, except in his desire to help his audience think about the issues he writes about, even if his positions on those issues are radical, disturbing, and confrontational. "I've come to the realization," he maintains, "that many people have been reading literary fiction for the same reason they read mainstream fiction: for entertainment and a form of escape. I don't want to write books that provide people with that. I want books that challenge, anger, and possibly offend."[51]

CHAPTER 2

The Business of Fancydancing and Old Shirts and New Skins

Sherman Alexie's first published work, *The Business of Fancy-dancing* (1992), is an eighty-four-page collection of poems and short stories, which, despite its brevity, received effusive praise from such reviewers as Leslie Ullman, who describes the collection as a "soft-blended tapestry of humor, humility, pride and metaphysical provocation out of the hard realities that make up its material."[1] As a poet, Alexie has much in common with such poets of the confessional school as Robert Lowell, Sylvia Plath, and John Berryman, who often wrote semi-autobiographical poems that expressed their innermost, frequently tormented feelings. However, unlike the confessional poets, who often lopsidedly focused on their personal sufferings, Alexie's poems run the gamut of human emotions: from drunken rage to playful humor and biting sarcasm, love poems and songs. It is difficult not to read many of Alexie's poems as autobiographical, as they often are situated on the Spokane Indian Reservation, where Alexie grew up, and also detail some of his actual life, such as the death of his sister and his odd jobs in Seattle. Still, many of Alexie's poems are definitely fictional and frequently blur the line between fiction and reality. Ultimately, Alexie leaves it unclear as to whether his poetry should be read as autobiographical, especially since he repeatedly stresses the importance of imagination. Rather, he seems to enjoy creating and maintaining a disequilibrium between fact and fiction, thereby never allowing the reader to feel that he is fully comprehensible through his writing. Furthermore, a good many of Alexie's poems contain elements of magic realism in which he places many historical figures, celebrities, and film characters—from Crazy Horse and Custer to Rocky and Robert De Niro—in the setting of the reservation.

Clever paradoxes and a common duplicity run throughout *The Business of Fancydancing.* There is humor in the pathos and pathos in the humor; there is anger tempered by pride, as well as desperation and poverty tempered by humor and affection. Just as it is often difficult to separate fact from fiction in Alexie's work, it is sometimes difficult to ascertain whether he is being serious or comic. It is not Alexie's intention to portray reservation Indians as helpless, poverty-stricken alcoholics, although many of his characters possess those characteristics. Rather, Alexie portrays reservation Indians as battered but resilient survivors of an unacknowledged American genocide, who continually struggle against the culture that stripped them of property, pride, and their indigenous culture.

Ambiguity immediately appears in the title poem of the collection, "The Business of Fancydancing." Fancydancing is a traditional form of Native American dance that allows a single dancer to display his or her skill or cunning. At the same time, it is a staged performance. The fancydancer is sly, intelligent, and surreptitious, able to outwit his oppressors. The modifier *business* suggest a colder economic reality, as if the fancydance itself has deteriorated from a high cultural art into a cold, economic necessity, possibly commodified by Western culture. It suggests that what was once an art has become a business, and that the fancydancer, in this case the individual engaging in what should

be a cherished, valued, cultural act, is using it for selfish aggrandizement, a kind of masquerade for money.

Indeed, this is what occurs in the poem, in which the narrator drives his friend, Vernon Wildshoe, a champion fancydancer,
from powwow to powwow solely in order to win money, not
out of a desire to display cultural pride or connect with other
Indian tribes. The two use the money mostly to buy alcohol or,
as Alexie notes, "a case of empty / beer bottles shaking our foun-
dations, we / stop at a liquor store, count out money, / and would
believe in the promise / of any man with a twenty."[2] However,
Alexie does not ultimately criticize these characters who engage
in this behavior, in part because they have little choice, being
nearly destitute: "We / got our boy, Vernon Wildshoe, to fill our
empty / wallets and stomachs, to fill our empty / cooler. Vernon
is like some promise / to pay the light bill, a credit card we / Indians get to use" (69).

In place of cultural traditions lies the struggle for economic
survival. Vernon's dances are motivated by sheer financial necessity more than greed, leading the narrator and Vernon to perceive the powwow and the fancydance as merely a means to an
end, without intrinsic worth other than potential economic profit.
The narrator notes, "Every drum beat is a promise / note written in the dust, measured exactly." The drum is the central instrument in Indian music, which itself is extremely important in
Indian culture, and thus if every drum beat is worthless, rubbed
out by the wind and people, then so is a significant portion of
Indian culture. Rather than focusing on the spiritual aspects of
the dance, the narrator portrays himself as internally depleted:
"Money is a tool, putty to fill all the empty spaces." The search
for money itself has become "a fancydance to fill where it's

empty," and presumably will not fill anything except their stomachs (69).

Similarly, in the story "Special Delivery," Alexie decries the deterioration of imagination and storytelling on the reservation. Typically, storytellers are among the most celebrated individuals in Indian tribes and culture. As Diane Niatum explains, "The values of the tribe are fused into the songs and stories. This is the case because the tribal poet believes that the word, if used respectfully, is invested with power and magic. Furthermore, this sense of a word's power was so commonplace among the tribes in the past that most believed the poem or story had a life of its own independent of the narrator."[3] Furthermore, Lois Einhorn argues that

> Native People view words as living, breathing, dynamic beings. Living beings create sound vibrations. When people breathe, they exchange spirits, and their breath transforms sounds into words. Uttered sound vibrations possess physical and spiritual energies that find their expression in the voices and visions of all sentient beings. . . . To Native People, then, words affirm existence. They breathe and beat, pound and palpitate, resound and reverberate. Words pulsate with life, making their use potent and powerful.[4]

Whereas traditionally Native cultures regard the storyteller as invested with special powers, in "Special Delivery," the primary reservation storyteller, Thomas Builds-the-Fire, is a social outcast. This is not to suggest that Thomas is necessarily a gifted storyteller, deserving of admiration and praise. In fact, one of the reasons he is ostracized is that the stories he tells are monotonous, self-indulgent, autobiographical repetitions or variations of the same story. In that, Thomas is a product of the imaginatively starved reservation. As Alexie explains:

> Thomas Builds-the-Fire told his story to every other Skin on the Spokane Indian Reservation before he was twelve years old. By the time he was twenty, Thomas had told his story so many times all the other Indians hid when they saw him coming, transformed themselves into picnic benches, small mongrel dogs, a 1965 Malibu with no windshield. Eventually, Thomas could only find audience with the half-assed Indians, passed out behind the tribal trading post. (39)

Storytelling has also become an empty, daily ritual for Thomas, which really has no larger purpose other than giving him an exaggerated sense of self-importance. "Thomas Builds-the-Fire woke up at precisely 6:30 every morning," Alexie writes, "stood in front of his bathroom mirror and repeated his story, practiced the words again and again. *This is my small ceremony,* Thomas thought as he dressed, combed his hair into braids, washed his face" (39). Furthermore, Thomas has misguided notions of his own abilities as a storyteller. Rather than trying to communicate clearly to others who live on the reservation, he sends his stories to "congressmen, game show hosts, invited the president of the United States to his high school graduation" (39).

Thomas's static daily routine mirrors the static monotony of the reservation, where other Indians engage in their own unimaginative routines of drinking or watching the automatic door of the trading post open and close for hours on end, as does one reservation Indian, Junior. Life on the reservation has become so dull that it has atrophied Thomas's and the other residents' imaginations and their hopes for the future. A series of unusual events beginning with Simon, another reservation Indian, knocking down a pole with his car, upsets the stasis of reservation life. When a tribal cop questions Simon, Thomas is visibly shaken by the change to his daily routine. "This isn't right, this isn't right, Thomas was chanting to himself when the tribal cop dropped Simon, unconscious to the dust" (43). When the tribal cop threatens Thomas, Thomas is not physically frightened as much as he is bewildered by the psychological change the incident forces upon him: "Thomas closed his eyes, not in fright, but in the hope that he would find something familiar when he opened them again" (44).

After running away and barricading himself in the post office, Thomas comes to an almost inadvertent epiphany about the importance of imagination, telling the tribal cops that he has a gun when in fact he has none. When the cops call his bluff, Thomas yells out, "Maybe I got the idea of a gun, and that's just as good" (45). Here, Thomas realizes how imaginative abilities can be powerful in transforming otherwise bleak or desperate situations. This revelation has an immediate effect upon Thomas who, afterward, while barricaded in the post office, thinks up and tells a new story to Eve, the postmistress. At the same time, Thomas tells Eve about the end of his story in which his "vision animal" tells him that he doesn't have "a dream that will come true" (47). Thomas's problem—as Eve notes at the end of the story by thinking, "It isn't necessary" (47)—is that it isn't necessary to have a dream that will come true. Rather, it is the dream itself or the imagination that is intrinsically important, rather than any tangible by-products that may result because of it. This is what Thomas realizes when he wields the idea of a gun: imagination can be as important or powerful as "reality."

In *The Business of Fancydancing,* Alexie exhibits a love/hate relationship with the reservation, more specifically a love for the strength of its residents, who struggle to survive amidst abysmal, nearly Third World conditions. However, he condemns the conditions themselves and how those conditions often poison or demolish pride and dignity. Alexie details the desperation of reservation life at the same time as he notes how the impoverished conditions help forge a strong community. It is a community that is held together by what destroys it (alcohol and poverty) and what helps it survive (humor and television) in a dangerous, almost destructive symbiosis. For instance, in the poem "Traveling," the narrator, on a bus with a basketball team in the Northwest, sees community, homogenization, and desperation in the towns he passes: "All the Indians in the bars drinking their culture or boarded up in their houses so much in love with cable television" (13).

Despite having no money and little food, the narrator and his father find humor in their bleak situation as a means to cope with poverty. When the narrator only finds two slices of bread in the whole van, he asks his father:

"Hey Dad, we ain't got any food left."

"What's in your hand?"

"Just two slices of bread."

"Well, you can have a jam sandwich, enit?"

"What's that?"

"You just take two slices of bread and jam them together."

(13)

Similarly, Alexie is humorous when detailing poverty on the reservation, as in the poem "Futures," a semisarcastic romanticization of the speaker's (or Alexie's) childhood on the reservation. The poem begins with an epigraph that reads, "oh children, think about the good times." In response to the epigraph, Alexie writes, "We lived in the HUD house / for fifty bucks a month. Those were the good times." Despite the fact that they were all unemployed, "we could always eat / commodity cheese and beef." No doubt this is not "the good life" as most Americans would consider it, but it is not complete devastation, for the end of the poem indicates that their family structure remains intact: "That was the summer I found / a bag full of real silver dollars / and gave all my uncles all / my brothers and sisters each one / and no one spent any no one" (35).

In other poems about cultural life on the reservation, Alexie displays the resilience of reservation traditions. In "Powwow," amidst the celebrations, the speaker notes "today, nothing has died, nothing / changed beyond recognition / dancers still move in circles" (52). At the same time, some cultural traditions have been polluted or tainted by the often obnoxious presence of various non-Indians, who do not attempt to understand the culture they witness but rather regard it as mere spectacle or entertainment. In the same poem, Alexie writes, "the fancydancers wear bells, you know / so they can't sneak up on white tourists" (51), suggesting that the presence of non-Natives has watered down and weakened Native cultural traditions.

Still, Alexie typically regards the problems on the reservation with biting humor. In the impoverished environment of the reservation, "love" doesn't exist in its traditional form. While this might make for a serious, tragic poem, Alexie presents it as tragicomedy. The speaker tells his "beloved": "I can meet you / in Springdale buy you beer / & take you home / in my one-eyed Ford / I can pay your rent on HUD house get you free / food from the BIA / get your teeth fixed at IHS" (58).

In other poems, Alexie appears disillusioned by the commodification and deterioration of Indian cultural life. In "Spokane

Tribal Celebration, September 1987," the speaker, while at a powwow, claims that "I want to believe every campfire / is a heart, every dollar bill a fire / that burns at the fingertips" (74). That the speaker *wants* to believe this suggests that he is not entirely convinced that the participants have genuine intentions and implies that there is something impure or missing from the celebration. That impurity or pollution is in part a result of alcohol abuse. The speaker's drunk friend, Seymour, calls alcohol his "bottle of dreams," and his and the other Indians' incessant drinking atrophies their imaginative abilities. A drunk Seymour claims that he can fly, but the realistic narrator notes that, "the only time Indian men / get close to the earth is when Indian men / pass out and hit the ground" (74). Yet the speaker does not ultimately pass judgment upon Seymour or any of the other drunk Indians, including himself, because the speaker is conflicted about drinking. While he acknowledges alcohol's potential to be destructive, he also considers it to be a possibly necessary means of self-protection: "I / wonder if I and the other Indian men / will drink all night long, if Seymour's dreams / will keep him warm like a blanket, like a fire" (74). Of course, the speaker has already established that Seymour's delusional alcoholic dreams are unrealizable, but at the same time that doesn't mean that his "dreams," deluded though they may be, will not somewhat sustain him.

The reservation, bleak as it may be, is still a stable, important home for the speaker of the poems, the characters portrayed, and Alexie himself because of strong communal and tribal ties. In "Gravity," Alexie claims that despite everything, most Indians still maintain a sense of ethnic identity and community, and that they will remember every person they meet of their own ethnicity because "every Indian has the blood of the tribal memory circling his heart. The Indian, no matter how far he travels away, must come back repeating, joining the reverse exodus" (80).

Still, if the Native American world that Alexie portrays in *The Business of Fancydancing* is conflicted, it is in part due to massive identity crises many experience due to being biracial. Alexie, in the seemingly autobiographical poem "13/16," addresses his own conflicted multiracial status, being three-sixteenths white. It begins as an angry renunciation of his white heritage with the lines: "I cut myself into sixteen equal pieces / kept thirteen and fed the other three / to the dogs" (16). The poem turns into an indictment of the dehumanization of Indians on reservations by the government, which enumerates them while determining and cataloging their identity. Alexie calls this process "reservation mathematics," with his own constituency determined by "father (full blood) + mother (5/8) = son (13/16)" (16). The dehumanizing process includes federal enrollment and leads to the final categorization and documentation in museums and in "roadside attractions / totem poles in Riverfront Park" (16). Finally, to add insult to injury, whites appropriate Indian culture. Alexie represents this in the poem with a ten-year-old white boy, who asks if the narrator "was a real Indian. He did not wait / for an answer, instead carving his initials / into the totem with a pocketknife: J.N." (16–17). The boy literally overwrites Indian culture, but metaphorically his act represents how mainstream Americans have rewritten "history" according to their own skewed perspective of Manifest Destiny and used the land for their own devices, leaving Indians without a clear identity, symbolically represented by the speaker (presumably Alexie) in the guise of the community cans "without labels." However, the speaker's father is not fooled by the outward appearance of these nameless cans, and he "opened them / one by one, finding a story in each" (17). To a large extent, this is also Alexie's purpose: to counteract the loss of identity and dehumanization by telling stories that provide a sense of identity, pride, and meaning.

As with other assimilated cultures, in Indian cultures there is also a trend for the younger generations to renounce or avoid their native culture. "Translated from the American" concerns a narrator and his mother who are traveling to the Spokane Tribal Celebration. His mother is uncomfortable with the narrator's son (her grandson) because he is half-white. She talks to her son in her native language, Salish, even though he doesn't understand it, and she refuses to say her grandson's name in English. The narrator is a college-educated Indian who went away, learned another language, and has become assimilated.

Although this character has assimilated, other Alexie characters have no interest in mainstream American culture, content to remain in a nearly hermetically sealed environment. In the poem "November 22, 1983," Alexie illustrates how America's icons don't hold the same significance for some Indians on the reservation. On the twentieth anniversary of JFK's death, the speaker's mother recalls that when she and her husband heard the original news of Kennedy's death, the speaker's father "changed / the channel to some station / still playing music / & he asked me to dance" (30). The narrator's father does not identify or look up to Kennedy, as American governmental politics have little importance on the reservation. For Alexie the reservation often feels like a country within a country, the culture of its residents extremely foreign to that of mainstream America. He writes in "Powwow": "Did you ever get the feeling / when speaking to a white American / that you needed closed captions?" (51). Still, that difference can appear in reservation Indians, whom Alexie often portrays as feeling inadequate in context with others, mainly whites. For instance, in "Indian Boy Love Song (#3)," the speaker describes how his cousin passionately kisses him after he tells her "she was more beautiful / than any white girl / I had ever seen" (56).

One aspect of Western culture that Alexie and others on the reservation wholeheartedly embrace is sports—more specifically, basketball. Only through sports, it seems, can some on the reservation achieve significant self-worth or self-esteem. However, any glory from sports is often transitory and fleeting. In "Love Hard," a nameless person tells the speaker about his father's alcohol problems but that he was also an excellent basketball player. The nameless person tells the speaker that his father knew how to "love hard" (31), but the product of his lifestyle is disillusionment and alcoholism, since his father cannot achieve the same level of pride and esteem as a typical reservation Indian—let alone in mainstream America—that he did as a star basketball player. In "Sudden Death," the speaker describes his father, living now "in the tin shack / where the television keeps the walls / breathing" (27), terminally haunted by a field goal he missed in 1956. In "Native Hero," a basketball hero, Reuben, becomes obsessively attached to the game, with "the basketball he keeps / tucked under his arm more gently / than any baby he may have fathered" (73). Although Alexie usually champions basketball on the reservation in these poems, it does not permanently transform anybody's life.

A more fruitful approach, which Alexie takes to empower reservation Indians, is to transform history by placing historical figures in contemporary contexts. At the same time, these figures, like Crazy Horse, aren't always meant to be accurate representations of their historical personages (which in itself is difficult to determine). Rather, they often symbolize aspects of Native culture or mainstream America. Alexie chooses Crazy Horse as an archetypal Indian symbol for his unrelenting desire to defend Native lands and culture as well as his defeat of Custer and his army at the Battle of Little Bighorn in 1876. In several of the poems, Alexie imagines Crazy Horse reincarnated in contemporary society, but as a person who has lost his cultural and ethnic pride as well as his revolutionary fervor. He does this to show how the spirit of Crazy Horse has vanished for most contemporary Indians, whom, he suggests, have grown complacent. Alexie envisions a contemporary Crazy Horse in "War All the Time" as an alcoholic Vietnam veteran who sells his medals. When the bartender "asks him why / he's giving up everything he earned, / Crazy Horse tells him you can't stop a man / from trying to survive, no matter where he is" (65). Revolutionary fervor, Alexie suggests, has become difficult, if not impossible, due to the struggle for economic survival. In another poem ("Missing"), Alexie portrays Crazy Horse as a beleaguered 7-Eleven worker who decides his dreams have "expired, have become so old they must be sent back to the distributor, recycled and shipped to another city" (71). Whereas, in subsequent writings, Alexie would have decried this character's resignation, here he accepts it as a necessity. Still, Alexie suggests that popular culture or television has transformative possibilities on the reservation, as it serves as one of the main determinants of identity. Thus, he envisions Crazy Horse as a television producer in "No Drugs or Alcohol Allowed." Crazy Horse "came / back to life / and started his own cable television channel and began the / reeducation / of all of us who spent so many years / skinless, driving our cars straight off cliffs directly into / the beginning of nowhere" (68).

Still, the seemingly pessimistic Alexie insists that Crazy Horse dreams are "the kind that don't come true" (72). The chimeras they provide lead both to salvation and to destruction in the sense that they provide hope but also lead people to ignore their problems or become monomaniacally involved in the pursuit of something unrealizable or virtually worthless, like the narrator's father "who lost a gold tooth in the forty-sixth wreck of his life / somewhere in Ford Canyon / and he spends a few hours every week with a metal detector, / scanning the ground / for that missing part, the part that came out whole and bloodless, / but fills you up with how much it stays gone" (72). Metaphorically, this character rather needlessly searches for a part of himself that he can't recover. Yet there is also humor in Alexie's depiction of Crazy Horse. Desperate for money, the narrator donates blood in the poem "Giving Blood," telling the nurse he's Crazy Horse. After a series of questions, the narrator is rejected by the white nurse who says: "I'm / sorry Mr. Crazy Horse / but we've already taken too much of your blood / and you won't be eligible / to donate for another generation or two" (78).

The antithesis of Crazy Horse in the collection is Buffalo Bill, who represents corrupt Western materialism and consumerism. Indeed, "by his own count, he [Buffalo Bill] killed 4,280 head of buffalo in seventeen months."[5] In the biting poem "Evolution," Alexie reincarnates Buffalo Bill as an amoral, contemporary capitalist. He opens up a pawnshop on the reservation "and the Indians come running in with jewelry / television sets, a VCR, a full-length beaded buckskin outfit / it took Inez Muse 12 years to finish" (48). Alexie continues to show how whites prey on impoverished Indians while showing Indians to be either greedy or desperate.

The Indians / pawn their hands, saving their thumbs for last, they pawn / their skeletons, falling endlessly from the skin /

and when the last Indian has pawned everything / but his heart, Buffalo Bill takes that for twenty bucks / closes up the pawn shop, paints a new sign over the old / calls his venture THE MUSEUM OF NATIVE AMERICAN CULTURES / charges the Indians five bucks a head to enter. (48)

Here, Alexie provides an account of how Indian culture has been mainly destroyed, bought, and commodified by mainstream America.

Old Shirts and New Skins

In *The Business of Fancydancing*, Alexie offers no specific ideas on to how to combat the vicious circle of impoverishment, depletion, and commodification. While in that collection he is normally descriptive and often despondent, with his next collection, *Old Shirts and New Skins* (1993), published by the American Indian Studies Center at the University of California, Los Angeles, Alexie is more assertive and direct as well as historically and culturally cognizant. The title represents Alexie's new attitude as "skins" is an affectionate moniker that Alexie and other Indians often call one another. His newfound optimism can be found in the poem "Drought," in which he writes: "Once I wrote of dreaming of a country / where three inches of rain fell in an entire year. / Then, I believed it was a way / of measuring loss. Now, I believe / it was a way of measuring how much / we need to gain."[6] In the preface to the collection, Paiute writer Adrian C. Louis praises the collection and Alexie as one of the few Indian writers who "speak to the condition of the majority of our Indian people" as opposed to maintaining the "sometimes romantic, sometimes halting caricatures on the silver screen" (viii). Furthermore, Louis describes Alexie as a visionary and claims that he "speaks in a voice that contains ancient wisdom and the fresh spontaneity of today's youth" (viii).

Alexie's development from being primarily a descriptive, passive poet to more of an active poet first appears in the epigraph to the collection, credited to one of Alexie's fictional characters, Lester FallsApart: "Poetry = Anger × Imagination." Whereas in *The Business of Fancydancing,* Alexie championed the use of any aspect of the imagination, here he suggests that art, or at least significant art, is a symbiosis of imagination coupled with anger. In other words, mere creativity is not enough; it must be fueled by an outrage, and for Alexie that outrage is primarily the historical treatment and current marginalization of American Indians by mainstream, predominantly white Americans. For Alexie, imagination or creativity fueled by anger can counteract the effects of outrage by offering hope or by aggressively challenging the status quo. In order to challenge mainstream culture, one needs to be passionately, even furiously inspired.

Although Alexie believes in the power of literature as an empowering tool, he does not overemphasize or exaggerate its importance. For instance, the poem "Native American Literature" is in part an indictment of lesser Indian writers who capitalize on Indian culture while ignoring the serious problems involved in reservation life. Alexie addresses these writers at the beginning of the poem: "You scour the reservation landfill / through the debris of so many lives: / old guitar, basketball on fire, pair of shoes / All you bring me is an empty bottle" (3). Alexie counters this by asking, "Am I the garbageman of your dreams?" (3). In other words, unlike other writers of Native American literature, Alexie is willing and believes it necessary to ground himself in the mire of reservation life. At the same time, he denies that Native American literature can forge any vast transformative changes: "It will not save you / or talk you down from the ledge / of a personal building" (3). The poem also criticizes what Alexie believes to be static monotony in contemporary Native American literature, exemplified by stereotypes and generalizations: "Often, you need a change of scenery / It will give you one black and white photograph" (4). For Alexie, much of Native American literature has become too superficial, too concerned with noting surface rather than substance in Indian culture. It "talks too much about the color / of its eyes and skin and hair." Furthermore, the poem suggests that there have been recent developments and changes in Native American literature: "Send it a letter: the address will keep changing. Give it a phone call: busy signal" (4). Ultimately, Alexie wants the reader to view Native American literature as a collaborative endeavor in which the reader has to meet the writer halfway, in which the reader is actively involved in making meaning: "In the end, it will pick you up from the pavement / & take you to the tribal café for breakfast. / It will read you the menu. / It will not pay your half of the bill" (5).

As he did in the poem "13/16" in *The Business of Fancydancing,* Alexie continues to fault the reservation itself and the process of enrollment as fundamentally confining and degrading on both physical and mental levels. With the poem "Architecture," Alexie establishes a further connection or cause-and-effect relationship between the physical layout of the reservation and the mental confinement it helps produce. He writes, making reference to the paltry, monotonous HUD houses ubiquitous on the reservation: "Foot by foot, / we measure definitions / assigned to us by years." The bleak conditions drive the residents into a meager consumerism, scrounging for survival, "where hands are the weapon, pressed / tightly against its heartbeat, breaking us /

down into everything we want to own" (7). Sadly, most residents don't want to own anything except the means to temporarily escape from their despondency through alcohol. Alexie demonstrates this in the poem "Economics of the Tribe," whose title is an oxymoron in the sense that the poem details how the economics of the individual, or the desire of the individual to improve his/her well-being, have supplanted any desire to better the lot of the tribe or reservation. The poem begins, "solvent means having enough money / to get drunk in Springdale again / means the checks came in." Since saving "means putting money away / for the weekend or powwow," it is doubtful that many have any long-term plans. Rather, they appear focused on achieving immediate gratification and have not incorporated traditional Western capitalist ideology, for Alexie describes them as "carrying it all in our pockets / passing it out at powwows" (8).

In *Old Shirts and New Skins,* Alexie focuses more on the boundaries between the white and Indian world and that of mainstream America and the reservation than in *The Business of Fancydancing.* In the poem "Powwow Polaroid," Alexie describes how a white tourist metaphorically tries to steal Indian culture by taking a picture of the fancydancers. "She took the picture, the flashbulb burned, and none of us could move," he writes. "The crowd panicked. Most fled the stands, left the dancers not dancing and afraid. The white woman with the camera raised her arms in triumph" (43). That this one small act ends up destroying the powwow shows the fragility of this ceremony. Alexie puts Indians on a moral pedestal by ending the poem with the speaker's uncle calling for forgiveness, which is how Indians have traditionally responded to cultural theft.

At the same time, what tears individuals and the reservation apart also brings them together: alcohol. In "Sundays, Too," an homage to Robert Hayden's "Those Winter Sundays," Alexie describes how drinking has become a new ritual on the reservation. He recalls a summer "all of us Indians drank the same kind of beer. At first, it was coincidence, economics. Then, it grew into a living thing, evolved and defined itself, became a ceremony, a tribal current, a shared synapse." The act becomes even more intimate as time elapses: "After hours of this drinking, only a few beers remained, the Indians shared, drank from the same can, bottle" (47). However, the optimism with which Alexie ends this poem—"There is nothing we cannot survive"—is counteracted by other poems about Alexie's own struggles with alcohol. In "Drought," he writes: "So many Indians born with the alcohol spirit / and I'm no different. My heart still / staggers when I feel the next drink / touch my lips" (75). When recalling his alcoholic father, Alexie blames vodka, "which stole his dreams / without scent" (75). In interviews, Alexie has said that he stopped drinking right after learning that his first poetry collection would be published, but some of these poems presumably predate that occurrence and suggest that Alexie might have followed in his father's footsteps had he continued drinking, evidenced by how he describes himself in "Poem" as an "alcoholic Jekyll and Hyde . . . drowning myself on a trail of beers" (77). In "The Unauthorized Biography of Lester FallsApart," Alexie describes another casualty of alcoholism and the bleak reservation: the homeless, alcoholic Lester, who, despite being awarded the Purple Heart for his service in Vietnam, has become emotionally and spiritually deadened. To Lester, there is no real difference between Vietnam and the reservation: "In your mind / Vietnam and the reservation / fancydance together" (50). Lester barely subsists on his military pension and by carrying groceries for old women, ultimately squandering his money on alcohol.

Still, Alexie does not pass judgment on Lester, but rather concludes: "*he survives / this way*" (52, italics in original).

As in *The Business of Fancydancing*, in *Old Shirts and New
Skins* Alexie resurrects historical figures such as Crazy Horse and
puts them in a contemporary setting, but, in the poems within
this collection, the resurrected figure is more defiant. In "Indian
Education," Alexie envisions Indian culture as being classified
and parceled into museums as historical relics. For Alexie, Crazy
Horse represents the epitome of Indian individuality and defi-
ance, and in this poem he imagines Crazy Horse coming back to
life "in a storage room in the Smithsonian" (19). The poem is
entitled "Indian Education," but it could more appropriately be
called "Indian Brainwashing" in the sense that Crazy Horse is
taken home by a security guard who leaves him to watch cable
television, in particular "every black and white / western, a
documentary about a scientist / who traveled the Great Plains in
the 1800s / measuring Indians and settlers, discovering / that the
Indians were two inches taller / on average" (19). Westerns, of
course, provide stereotypical depictions of Indians, and the documentary trivializes larger issues. With this poem, Alexie demonstrates how Indians often derive a sense of heritage, culture, and
identity through the distortions of mainstream American television.

Alexie has Crazy Horse take on more of an active role in
"Crazy Horse Speaks." Specifically, Crazy Horse defiantly speaks
out against his historical marginalization. Alexie views him as a
historic liberator, a martyr even, for Indian independence and
self-defense, even though many consider him to be the savage
leader who massacred Custer's army at the Battle of the Little
Bighorn. Considering his categorization, Crazy Horse angrily
describes himself as "sleeping between / the pages of dictionaries

/ your language cuts / tears holes in my tongue / until I do not have strength to use the word *Love*" (62, italics in original). Alexie has Crazy Horse explain that he and Sitting Bull fought against invading whites because they were resisting being enslaved by them: "I sat across the fire / from Sitting Bull / shared smoke and eyes. / We both saw the same thing / our futures tight and small / an 8 × 10 dream / called the reservation. / We had no alternatives / but to fight again and again / live our lives on horse-back." Furthermore, Crazy Horse criticizes his unmerited label of *Crazy,* claiming instead that his identity has been tarnished by mainstream Americans, who are unable or unwilling to comprehend him: "I am the mirror / practicing masks / and definitions. / I have always wanted to be anonymous / instead of the crazy skin / who rode his horse backward / and laid down alone" (62).

Alexie's sympathies and admiration clearly lie with Crazy Horse, not with his historical nemesis, General George Armstrong Custer, who for Alexie represents a cold, merciless, violent American mentality and whom Alexie displays as a vicious, cold-blooded murderer. Toward that end, the poem "Custer Speaks" begins with an epigraph from Custer at the age of seven: "My voice is for war!" Furthermore, Alexie's Custer is blood-thirsty and possibly psychotic, proudly proclaiming, "Listen: every part of me is for battle" (36). Alexie's Custer uses ridiculous rationalizations to defend his massacre of Indians, his orders to shoot fleeing women and children because "they had to be removed to make Kansas, the West, safe. They were barriers to progress. You call it genocide; I call it economics" (37). Ultimately, Alexie views Custer as a symbol for mass destruction and for war itself. He concludes the poem with: "I was born again in Hiroshima. / I was born again in Birmingham. / . . . I was born again in Saigon. / I was born again in Iraq" (38).

Whereas "Custer Speaks" is at least partly sarcastic, making it somewhat difficult to take Alexie's accusations seriously, "Postcards to Columbus" is an angry, accusatory poem aimed at those who celebrate the "discovery" of North America, which for Alexie and many other Indians represents the beginning of their cultural, collective, and individual decline as well as the start of a centuries-long campaign of massacre and colonization. For Alexie and many other Indians, Columbus's "discovery" is more like an invasion. Alexie insists, "Christopher Columbus, you are the most successful real estate agent / who ever lived, sold acres and acres of myth." For Alexie, the "myth" involves a convoluted belief in Manifest Destiny, that American settlers possessed a God-given dictate to possess as much of the land of North America as possible. In response to the celebrations planned for 1992, Alexie proclaims that his tribe will "honor the 500th anniversary of your invasion, Columbus, by driving blindfolded cross-country / naming the first tree we destroy *America*. We'll make the first guardrail / we crash through our national symbol. Our flag will be a white sheet / stained with blood and piss" (41). For Alexie, at least in this poem, destruction and violence underlie the settling of the continent; Columbus and subsequent "explorers" ought to be vilified, not celebrated for their deeds.

While Alexie's attitude toward America appears rather unrelenting in "Postcards to Columbus," he is more ambivalent in the poem "Vision (2)." Here, although Alexie criticizes Americans for narcissistically believing in their superiority, he also praises aspects of American culture. The poem begins with the speaker riding to the top of the highest building in Spokane. From that vantage point, he claims to see "500 years of America: *Over 1 Billion Illusions Served*" (27, italics in original).

However, Alexie immediately counters criticism of America with praise for its kitsch and convenience: "There is so much of this country I love, its supermarkets and bad television, the insane demand of a dollar bill in my pocket, fireworks celebrating the smallest occasions. I am happy I can find a cup of hot coffee 24 hours a day." Furthermore, Alexie questions his own gripes against mainstream America, considering that he hails from a tribe (Spokane) that "escaped many of the hardships other Native Americans suffered. By the time the 20th century reached this far west, the war was over. Crazy Horse was gone and the Ghost Dancers were only ghosts." That does not counteract his feelings of marginalization, however, as Alexie concludes that all Native Americans are "extras" in a narrative dominated by the white majority (27).

While Alexie may view Native Americans as solely extras in a country that caters to the white majority, he finds points of intersection and common ground to build upon between white, mainstream popular culture and Native American culture/history. The poem "Texas Chainsaw Massacre," for instance, is a homage to the movie of the same name that Alexie likes because it reminds him of violent atrocities committed against Indians. When watching the film, Alexie remembers "the killing grounds / of Sand Creek / where 105 Southern Cheyenne and Arapaho women and children / and 28 men were slaughtered by 700 heavily armed soldiers, / led by Chivington and his Volunteers. *Volunteers*" (44, italics in original). Ultimately, Alexie explains that he appreciates the movie because it speaks to his internalized rage as an American Indian who knows of the crimes committed and still being committed against other Indians and also because he, like most Americans, has been inundated with consumerism and violence: "This country demands that particular sort of weakness: / we must devour everything on our plates / and ask for more." Finally, he concludes that he values the movie "because I am an American / Indian and have learned / hunger becomes madness easily" (45). In essence then, the movie is important to Alexie because it reminds him not to become consumed by rage and anger and to be vigilant against that possibility. Likewise, Alexie uses such other popular American films as *Citizen Kane* and *The Godfather* and places them in the context of the reservation. He does this to reach a broader audience, as an important intersection between white and Native cultures. Furthermore, he realizes how popular culture, in particular film and television, has become the primary determinant of identity for all Americans, including Native Americans.

However, Alexie remains ambivalent when considering whether popular culture has the potential to help Indians and their communities. He insists that "The 20th century warrior relies / on HBO for his vision / at three in the morning" (55). However, Alexie does not think it possible to return to an Edenic pre-Western state of civilization, nor does he completely denigrate American popular culture. It is from popular culture that he can learn about people and the ways of the world: "Last night it was THE GODFATHER made me realize / how a slight gesture / can change the world, how the smallest facial tic can give the illusion of / perfection, by highlighting / imperfection" (55). While realizing that life in contemporary America is more a simulation than a reality and that what is accepted as "reality" is often illusory, he insists that "there are so many illusions I need to believe" (74). In doing so, Alexie doesn't put himself on a pedestal; an urban dweller, he cannot function without accepting the appearance of normalcy. If "Poetry = Anger × Imagination," as the epigraph to Alexie's collection insists, then the imaginative poetry Alexie writes may be the illusions he needs to believe in order to survive. In this collection, reality may be too painful for him to fully confront, for as Emily Dickinson writes, "Tell the truth but tell it slant / success in circuits lie / The truth must dazzle gradually / or every man be blind."

CHAPTER 3

First Indian on the Moon and *The Lone Ranger and Tonto Fistfight in Heaven*

With his next publication, *First Indian on the Moon* (1993)—a collection of poetry often alternating between short prose blurbs and free verse—Alexie's themes become more complex and at times ambiguous. If taken seriously, the title may allude to Alexie's commitment to use his imagination to help restore pride and self-worth to his reservation/tribe or to the larger Indian world by helping Indians reach a level of maximum inclusion in mainstream American society. At the same time, the title may also be a playful joke, alluding to the author's personal desire for individual transcendence. He may want to be considered as "the first Indian on the moon" in the sense of wanting to be recognized for expanding the boundaries of Native American literature, going where no Indian has gone before; thereby the title might be an attempt at self-promotion. Also, Alexie may be alluding to how he or other contemporary Indian artists or urbanities extend themselves into foreign territory (in this case, the moon represents the loftiest goals of white, mainstream America) vis-à-vis their exploration of the white world.

To be certain, Indians and whites (individually and culturally) interact and conflict considerably more in this collection than in the previous two, in terms of traditions, imagination, and personal relationships. Almost entirely absent is the roman-ticization of the reservation and its residents, which was present in both of Alexie's previous collections. For example, in the seemingly autobiographical "Influences," Alexie describes his or the speaker's alcoholic, neglectful parents who would often leave him and his sisters in the car while they would go out drinking, "emerging every half-hour with Pepsi, potato chips, and more promises."[1] The poem suggests that these early childhood experiences have helped influence the speaker's later mistrust. Yet Alexie downplays the pessimism by claiming, "This is not about sadness. This is about the stories / imagined / beneath the sleeping bags / between starts / to warm up the car" (9). In this poem, it isn't mainstream America or whites that produce disillusionment but rather the Indian world that does, as evidenced by the speaker's distrust of his parents (granted, a case could be made that the speaker's parents are the casualties of white, mainstream America, but such an explanation would unfairly absolve them of responsibility). Through these experiences, the speaker's imagination grows: "This is about the stories / I created / how I built / landscapes and imaginary saviors" (9). Instead of viewing the neglect and, along with it, his childhood as wholly damaging, the speaker believes that the emotional damage inflicted upon him also sparked his imagination and creativity.

This interrelated, almost paradoxical cause-and-effect relationship between damage/destruction and creation can also be seen in several poems in the collection concerning fire (rather than water, which was a recurring symbol in Alexie's first two collections). For Alexie, fire is both a literal, tangible force and a complex symbol representing destruction, passion, and creation, all of which are interrelated. In "Genetics" and the nine-part

"Fire Storm," he describes how he and his family have been repeatedly hurt by fire, which not only destroyed three of their cars in electrical fires and burned down their house but also killed his sister and brother-in-law, who both perished in a trailer fire. Yet this pain and destruction sparks Alexie's creativity and desire to come to grips with—or possibly make sense of—the seemingly senseless through poetry.

However, there is a cognizance on Alexie's part of his tendency to overdramatize or overuse fire as a destructive symbol or poetic topos. In "Fire Storm," when Alexie describes his sister's and brother-in-law's deaths, he admits that he uses the metaphor of fire in a self-serving manner, to bring significance and meaning to an otherwise meaningless act: "I give fire simple life and hate so I can assign exaggerated love and invent acts of heroism" (23). In this experimental metapoem, written in a Barthian postmodern style, Alexie writes: "We create metaphors to compensate for what we have lost. The fire did not crown over my head. The fire crowned above the head of a local news reporter who stopped tape [sic] and escaped." For Alexie, grief or destruction as manifested through fire can only be defeated or counteracted by making one's self strong enough to withstand the destruction. Thereby, in part 5 of the poem, the speaker describes himself as taking on attributes of fire, of internalizing it to counteract its destructive power. In this section, the speaker inhabits the fire storm: "My ribcage a barn fire / my hair a crown of flame" (24). Furthermore, Alexie uncovers the duplicity in the symbol, for fire sustains life just as it takes it away. The speaker recalls how his family would need to light a fire in order to warm up their house in the morning, and their resistance but eventual need to light the fire on the morning they learn of the death of Alexie's sister and brother-in-law by fire. At the end of the poem, Alexie concludes that the only way to come to grips with the pain and damage caused by the real or metaphoric fire (or the trauma it produces) is to relinquish attachments to possessions and possibly to people as well. In a Buddhist-like gesture, Alexie offers his possessions and self to the fire: "Here, I offer what I own, change / my references and gather ash / from the roads I've traveled. Heart / lost in a couch fire; heart fallen / to ash after the slight touch / of fear. . . . Here, I offer / what I own and what I don't own" (27). Only through this process, it seems, can Alexie come to grips with the tragedies he and his family have endured.

While this poem demonstrates Alexie's desire to use poetry to manage grief, that does not mean he strongly deviates from his poetic praxis, expressed in *Old Shirts and New Skins* as Poetry = Anger × Imagination. In this collection, his anger is often directed toward the meager quality of life on the reservation. In the prose poem "A Reservation Table of Elements," for instance, Alexie metaphorically demonstrates how deeply ingrained despondency has become on the reservation. The poem, broken into sections with natural elements (aluminum, hydrogen, neon, copper, and oxygen) as titles, displays how even the natural has turned destructive on the reservation. It is as if the natural world rebels against the unnatural, abysmal way of life on the reservation. In the section titled "Aluminum," one Indian loses his fingers when he dips a firecracker "into an empty Diet Pepsi and held the can until it exploded" (38). In the section titled "Neon," instead of neon illuminating anything, it serves to confuse fantasy and reality. As Victor, an overworked employee at a neon sign factory, claims, "I'm not sure anymore what's real and what ain't" (39). Other neon signs like "ALL TYPES OF LOANS CONSIDERED" turn out to be chimeras and the "BUY SELL

TRADE" neon sign and one outside a tavern lead the speaker toward despondency. In the section titled "Copper," the speaker recalls how the pipes froze during winter on the reservation, and in "Oxygen" there is an account of an Indian man who passed out and drowned in a mud puddle. Still, there are glimpses of life-affirming natural elements as a couple recalls how they fell in love in a tavern with a large overhanging neon sign, and the speaker vividly recalls the oxygen he breathes when kissing an Indian woman.

For Alexie there is a wide cultural gap between mainstream American culture and Native American culture. In "Year of the Indian," Alexie gives a month-by-month account of life on the reservation to show how little American traditions mean on the reservation or how they have been transformed. For January, Alexie does not describe a joyous New Year's celebration. Rather, there is an account of racial hatred as an old girlfriend confesses to the Indian speaker (presumably Alexie) that she hates Indians, apparently forgetting that her boyfriend (the speaker) is Indian. During February, there is the bleak thought that "Spring may never come" (11). In March, St. Patrick's Day is celebrated on the reservation merely because it provides them an excuse to drink. For April, Alexie suggests that Crazy Horse has become the Indian equivalent of Jesus Christ, writing, "How would your heart change if I told you Jesus Christ had already come back for the second time and got crucified again? He called himself Crazy Horse and never said anything about a third attempt." In May, presumably on Memorial Day, one Indian, Moses, wants to "memorialize every Indian who died in the war, fighting for this country and against this country during the last five hundred years" and uses swallows, releasing millions of them. He refuses to memorialize Americans who were killed in the war, preferring instead to create his own special memorial to Indians killed by Americans in what many, including Alexie, believe to be an unacknowledged genocide. There is little or no celebration on Independence Day in July; rather, "the air is heavy with smoke and whiskey" (12). The speaker and others on the reservation do not have anything to celebrate in their literally confined, cagelike existence on the reservation; therefore, the speaker insists, "all I want is a little piece of independence" (13). Labor Day also has no real meaning for the speaker who works in a Laundromat seven days a week for minimum wage: "Every day I feel dirty and used. I'm a dishrag, cloth diaper, mismatched sock."

American holidays also make the speaker feel further excluded from American society. During Halloween, a white child dressed as an Indian approaches the speaker, proudly proclaiming: "You're an Indian and I'm dressing up like an Indian for Halloween, too" (14–15). The speaker responds by whispering something threatening in the boy's ears. There is no real Thanksgiving on the reservation; for the November entry, the speaker wanders around "wondering where my family will find their food during the long winter" (14) and rejoicing when a fifty-pound bag of potatoes drops off the back of a truck that has lost its way in the reservation. At Christmas, it is Crazy Horse who dresses as Santa Claus, and the requests he gets aren't so much for presents as they are for a means of survival: "All the Indian boys and girls asking for jobs, college educations, a ticket for a Greyhound bus traveling back or ahead five hundred years. Crazy Horse searches his pack but he only finds a few hard candies, an orange, and miles and miles of treaties." The more privileged others "open their presents, all finding rifles, hammers and nails to build walls." With this ending, Alexie suggests that Indians on the reservation have internalized their confinement, imprisoned themselves mentally and spiritually.

If one problem Alexie identifies is the tendency for Indians to psychologically confine themselves (in part a by-product from physical confinement on the reservation or marginalization), he attempts to counteract confinement by intellectually challenging mainstream American frameworks. In "On the Amtrak from Boston to New York City," Alexie identifies conflicts between the perspectives of the dominant American majority and Indians. In this poem, while on a train, an elderly white woman points out to the speaker what she considers to be historical landmarks, houses that are over two hundred years old. Yet the woman considers historical landmarks from her culturally biased perspective while the speaker considers the many Indian traditions, sacred sites, and tribal stories "whose architecture is 15,000 years older than the corners of the house that sits / museumed on the hill" (79). Presumably, this woman and most Americans aren't aware of or concerned with sacred historical sites established and maintained by Natives prior to Western colonization of the Americas. While the woman eagerly looks for Walden Pond, it means little or nothing to the speaker, who is more concerned with a vast number of Native sacred sites that are not preserved. However, he does not criticize the woman directly: "I don't have a cruel enough heart to break / her own by telling her there are five Walden Ponds / on my little reservation out West / and at least a hundred more surrounding Spokane" (79). In that sense, the speaker abandons the attempt to bridge the gap in perspective, presumably giving up on the possibility for open communication. Rather, he promotes passive, surreptitious resistance, evidenced by the poem's last line: "Somebody from the enemy thought I was one of their own" (79). That he calls her the enemy indicates that he feels (at least in this instance) communication and bridging the gap between cultural perspectives is mostly futile.

Similarly, in "Apologies," the speaker decides not to confront a white person, the father of his current love interest, who expresses markedly different, even insulting viewpoints, in contrast to those of the speaker. This white individual "curses the suggestion that we owe Japan / an apology for Nagasaki and Hiroshima" (59). It is human nature, according to the speaker, to be polite and to repress outrage and dissension:

> All day, we check our hair
> in mirrors and mumble silent
> apologies for the ordinary.
> We say *Excuse me* to the fast food cashier
> when our dollar bills are wrinkled
> and *I'm sorry* to the tailor
> measuring across our body
> because of the proximity of our hearts.
> Jesus, these apologies begin
> with a whisper, then
> become a war. (61)

In other words, Alexie suggests that everyday courtesies can not only be disingenuous but destructive to ourselves and others because they force us to behave in a manner not conducive to our true feelings. The speaker's unlikely, half-baked solutions to avoiding pain and confrontation involve either diversion or mass acknowledgment of human suffering with "newspapers headlined PAIN" (60). Ultimately, the end result is that the speaker (and presumably Alexie as well) must learn to navigate a tightrope between acquiescence and anger. The speaker goes on to describe that when the father of his girlfriend "curses the suggestion / that we owe the Japanese / an apology for Nagasaki and Hiroshima, I want / to tell him 'It's all right / I understand' but I also want to strip him naked / and take photographs of his diseased skin / and I want to throw your father out the door / into the wheat fields, now snow fields / then killing fields." Hence the speaker concludes that he has been divided "into two halves" of rage and "civilized" repression. Complicating the matter is the fact that the speaker has no idea what to do with his rage and how it might be transformed into something productive.

Alexie, meanwhile, uses poetry precisely to transform rage or anger into something productive or constructive. One good example of this is "My Heroes Have Never Been Cowboys." In this poem, Alexie upsets stereotypical notions of the quintessential American icon of the heroic cowboy. He criticizes the skewed but commonly accepted history of the settlement of America as the beginning of real "American" history. Alexie writes, "Did you know that in 1492 every Indian instantly became an extra in the Great American Western?" (102). In other words, the metanarrative of early American settlers as rugged, heroic, freedom-loving people has generally been accepted as truth, when in reality it is at least partially a fiction. Furthermore, popular culture has inflated the image of the cowboy, who often appears almost superhuman and invincible: "On Saturday morning television, the cowboy has fifty bullets in his six-shooter; he never needs to reload. It's just one more miracle for this country's heroes." These "heroes," Alexie suggests, are not worthy of admiration, let alone deification. Whereas young white children often play the role of the cowboy in fighting games, Alexie points out that "on the reservation, when we played Indians and cowboys, all of us little Skins fought on the same side against the cowboys in our minds." In response to the deification of gun-toting cowboys, Alexie champions the power of intelligent, verbal, nonphysical violent resistance: "My heroes have never been cowboys; my heroes carry guns in their minds" (102). Rather than portraying them as cold-blooded murderers—which, Alexie argues, they ultimately are—the popular media characterizes cowboys as heroic in winning the "war" against the Indians and in fulfilling the creed of Manifest Destiny.

The deification of cowboys comes at a cost of denigrating Indians, and the influence of this paradigm can even be seen in the attitudes of Indians who live on the reservation. The speaker recalls, "Looking up into the night sky, I asked my brother what he thought God looked like and he said 'God probably looks like John Wayne'" (103). This is a wholly shocking statement considering that Wayne often fights against and/or kills Indians in his films. The speaker retorts, "We've all killed John Wayne more than once," but decries the lack of parity between the Western and Indian views of the settling of the country: "What about the reservation home movies? What about the reservation heroes?" (104). While it might seem that Alexie's purpose would be to create the equivalent of reservation home movies and reservation heroes, he ultimately regards the endeavor to be somewhat futile, unable really to counteract mainstream historical conceptions. He thereby concludes the poem by asserting to a friend, presumably another Spokane Indian writer named Arthur: "I have no words which can save our lives, no words approaching forgiveness, no words flashing across the screen at the reservation drive-in, no words promising either of us top billing. Extras, Arthur, we're all extras" (104).

If Indians are all extras in the great American historical and cultural narrative—written and directed mainly by whites—that

Alexie decries, they also buy into or are blanketed by dominant American popular culture. In several poems in "First Indian on the Moon," Alexie describes how popular films have come to usurp the importance of Native culture. For instance, after watching the movie *Rocky,* Yakima Indians obsessively play the movie theme song over and over again instead of playing traditional Indian music. In describing the overwhelmingly positive response to *Star Wars* on the reservation, Alexie is less laudatory, claiming that "They murder us too, these heroes we find in the reservation drive-in" (17). Alexie suggests that embracing popular-culture icons leads to the abandonment of cultural identity; Indians embrace white celebrities instead of those of their own ethnicity, which leads to homogenization and unconscious subservience. "Over and over," he writes, "we make these movies our own promises, imagine our fathers never lose, pretend our mothers slice their skin a hundred times in testament. Soon we will sit around old drums and sing songs: 'You promised us the earth and all we got was the moon.'" Alexie portrays mainstream American films as mostly unhealthy diversions for reservation Indians, who fully embrace these films and their protagonists rather than their own culture. In the section of the poem subtitled "Enter the Dragon," Alexie imagines an Indian boy emulating Bruce Lee but then poses the question: "But tell me, Mr. Lee, *what's the use*? There is no soundtrack for the rest of that Indian boy's life, no sudden change in music to warn him of impending dangers" (16). Rather, the film is only escapist, providing immediate diversion and temporary pleasure, but it does nothing to change the lives of Indians for the better. The only public figures or celebrities that Alexie embraces and places on the reservation in his magic-realist prose poems tend to be musicians/outsiders or actors typically known for playing outsiders, like Patsy Cline, Robert De Niro, and Marlon Brando. For Alexie, these individuals crystallize the Indian condition. By placing them in the literal context of the reservation, Alexie humanizes them for Indians.

For Alexie, the white and Indian world can never meet on entirely equal ground as there always is a power struggle of sorts involved. Specifically, interracial relationships serve as a microcosm of Indian-white relationships, and Alexie depicts them as ultimately a struggle for power. Several poems in *First Indian on the Moon* are addressed to a white woman, with whom Alexie was probably involved at the time. Alexie portrays their relationship often like a battle of conflicting forces, rather than a loving relationship. In "Spontaneous Composition," he writes: "Sometimes when an Indian boy loves / a white girl and vice versa / it's like waking up / with half the world / on fire. You don't know / if you should throw water / onto those predictable flames / or let the whole goddamn thing burn" (58). This poem suggests that there is an element of masochism involved in the relationship, as does the poem "Tiny Treaties." In this poem, the speaker tells the woman that what he remembers most about their relationship is having to hitchhike "fifteen miles through a blizzard / after my reservation car finally threw a rod / on my way back home from touching / your white skin again" (56). As he hitchhikes home, the speaker waits for white people to pick him up "for a brake light, that smallest possible treaty," but no one stops for him. For the speaker, this is a quintessential moment in which he realizes the daunting size of the chasm between whites and Indians and thereby realizes that there isn't significant trust between him and the woman. The speaker thinks he would have asked her if she would have picked him up if she didn't know him, but then he writes, "I won't ask you the question / because I don't want to know the answer" (57). Obviously, the speaker does not fully trust this woman with whom he is involved and yet he continues the relationship, possibly because he thrives on conflict and possibly because he lacks the self-esteem to consider himself worthy of affection, at least from this white woman.

However personal and often tormented these poems may be, Alexie also uses them as a means to inquire further into Indian-white relationships. Being involved with a white woman makes the speaker consider that he might have been somewhat unfairly vilifying non-Natives and romanticizing Indians. In "Seven Love Songs Which Include the Collected History of the United States of America," Alexie writes: "I blamed your arrogant grand-fathers / for the flames and you / blamed my grandfathers / and their predictable rage. Was it me who shot arrows / soaked in alcohol or was it you / who dropped another European match / without thought?" (60). Similarly, in "Blankets," the speaker, addressing a white woman, explains: "Because of you, I some-times believe the Ghost Dancers were only half right. It's true we need the buffalo back but we need the whites too" (68). However, one primary reason that Alexie or the speaker "needs" white people is that he thrives on conflict and dissension, espe-cially as a poet who has described anger as being a primary cata-lyst for his writing. He concludes the poem by explaining "At least, I need you / to cover me / like a good blanket / with warmth / and faith, / I need you to cover me / like a smallpox blanket / with anger and pain."

Despite the torment and grief it causes the speaker of many of Alexie's poems, Alexie suggests that interracial romance can be a form of racial progress, claiming that "My grandfathers and your grandfathers / would have hated each other, traded /

only insults and gunfire / but we choose to love" (62). However, the speaker perceives the outside world as interfering with their desire to become color-blind. When they go to restaurants, "As we waited to be seated / those familiar eyes stared / hateful and hurtful / from behind menus and newspapers" (63). That the relationship will probably not last appears evident in the last lines of the poem in which the speaker acknowledges how he has been duped into believing the goodwill and trustworthiness of the white world, despite what his experience tells him. Addressing the woman, he writes: *"After 500 years of continuous lies / I would still sign treaties for you"* (65, italics in original).

Still, while anger and pain provide some of Alexie's literary fuel, in this collection he broadens his perspective beyond that of Native Americans to other ethnic minorities. The title of the poem "The Game between the Jews and the Indians Is Tied Going into the Bottom of the Ninth Inning," suggests that Alexie sees Jews and Indians as similar, both historically oppressed minorities and victims of ethnic violence. There is common ground between the two ethnic groups, as Alexie acknowledges that "we are both survivors and children / and grandchildren of survivors" (80).

In another poem, Alexie considers how his strong, often combative views on race and ethnicity might be informed by living in an environment (Spokane) that is predominantly white, thereby making him and other minorities feel further marginalized. In "Because I Was in New York City Once and Have Since Become an Expert," Alexie wonders if he writes about race so much because he hails from a homogenous area that lacks ethnic diversity. He is taken aback when clerks in New York stores don't look at him with suspicion, presumably because they are accustomed to seeing people of all different creeds and colors.

Oddly, Alexie writes that "I almost missed Spokane, the city where I was born and which reminds me continually of my dark eyes and skin and hair" (81). For Alexie, constant awareness of his ethnicity is both a blessing and a curse. It is a blessing in the sense that it makes him more cognizant of his ethnic identity, but it is a curse in the sense that it denies him other avenues for nonethnic identity and compels him to be vigilant against attacks or discrimination. Furthermore, the experience of being oppressed fuels Alexie's outrage, which in turn informs his identity and his writing. Therefore, he wonders, "Could it be true? Am I Native American only when I am hated because of it? Does racism determine my entire identity?" If this is the case, then Alexie may not be able to function in a color-blind society (if there could ever be such a place), for to do so would mean nullifying his core identity.

Whereas in poems like "13/16" in Alexie's previous collections, he completely dismisses his white ancestry, proudly announcing that he is "tossing it to the dogs," in *First Indian on the Moon* he is more ambivalent about his mixed ancestry. He writes, "Mixed-up and mixed-blood / I sometimes hate / the white in me / when I see their cruelty / and I sometimes hate / the Indian in me / when I see their weakness / because I understand the cruelty and weakness in me. I belong to both tribes" (43). Whereas in *The Business of Fancydancing* and *Old Shirts and New Skins,* for the most part, Alexie wholeheartedly embraces the Indian community, in this poem he envisions the possibility of a postethnic space beyond race: "I've been dreaming of a life / with a new shape, somewhere / in the in-between / between tipi and HUD house / between magic and loss / I'm always dreaming / of a life between / the 3/16 that names me white / and the 13/16 / that names me Indian."

Still, this dream never takes exact shape, and it is within an Indian community or with other Indians that Alexie feels most at home and most included. For instance, in the poem "Freaks," the speaker encounters three Indians eating Spam and drinking from a wine bottle. Because of their shared ethnicity, he gives them some money, and their immediate comfort and rapport can be seen by how they call each other cousin and ask the speaker what tribe he is from. The poem is called "Freaks" because that is how Alexie believes these homeless, drunk Indians are perceived by most of the dominant white mainstream. In contrast, the speaker views the homeless Indians as distant relatives and clearly feels a connection to them because of their shared ethnicity. After the speaker gives them money, he comments: "I don't feel generous or guilty, just half-empty and all lonely in this city which would kill me as slowly as it is killing these three cousins of mine" (49). It is doubtful if not impossible that the speaker could experience the same connection and concern for white strangers. Thereby his preference for Indians remains intact. The ending of the poem shows this: "I say goodbye with handshakes and walk down the waterfront, passing by white tourists who don't care if they ever know my name. I walk all day, looking for just one more kind face." One reason that whites and Indians can't usually connect, Alexie suggests, is because most whites have not experienced marginalization and discrimination or the near constant state of vigilance that many minorities experience. For instance, in "Before We Knew about Mirrors," Alexie explains: "When an Indian stranger sees another Indian stranger, they both stare. They have the same eyes, mirrors, reflecting what they have witnessed; understanding the distance pain creates between past and present, they move toward random consolations" (50). Ultimately, the chasm between the

ethnic majority and minority groups can't fully be bridged,
Alexie suggests, because of institutionally unequal power structures, which allow the ethnic majority financial, cultural, and
educational privileges above and beyond that of minority groups.
First Indian on the Moon ultimately offers no formula for ethnic harmony, which, at least in this collection, Alexie believes to
be a chimera. Although it may be possible to approach equality,
it can never be fully realized.

The Lone Ranger and Tonto Fistfight in Heaven

Alexie's next collection, *The Lone Ranger and Tonto Fistfight in
Heaven* (1993), mostly composed of short stories, attracted a
larger audience than his first three collections. In a review of the
book for *American Indian Quarterly,* Denise Low claims that
the collection reads "like a casebook of postmodernist theory—
beyond surrealism and absurdity, and certainly beyond classi-
cism. Irony, pastiche, and mingling of popular cultures occur
throughout the book."[2] However, while there are multiple layers of significance and a good amount of parody and play in
the stories, Alexie is also a serious moral and ethical writer, committed to Native issues and to counteracting Indian oppression.
This is immediately evident in the title of the collection. James
Cox argues that the title displays deliberate subversion, in which
the traditionally subservient Indian Tonto refuses to serve in the
role set out for him, thereby challenging "the Lone Ranger, the
iconographic Western hero and the representative of the dominant culture."[3] Furthermore, Cox claims that "Alexie's characters are engaged in the same metaphorical fistfight as the titular
Tonto: they struggle for self-definition and self-representation
against the oppressive technological narratives that define
Native Americans as a conquered people, as decontextualized,

romanticized, subservient Tontos, and Native America as a conquered landscape."[4]

However, if Native America has indeed been "conquered," then Alexie shows how Indians have helped conquer themselves by self-defeating ideology. Nevertheless, Alexie is no fatalist, for he also suggests that Indians can counteract their oppression through imagination, hope, and self-sufficiency. The collection begins with a story, "Every Little Hurricane," in which the reservation Indians display self- and mutually destructive tendencies. "Although it was winter, the nearest ocean four hundred miles away, and the Tribal Weatherman asleep because of boredom," Alexie begins, "a hurricane dropped from the sky in 1976 and fell so hard on the Spokane Indian Reservation that it knocked Victor from bed and his latest nightmare."[5] This "hurricane" is actually a tribal New Year's Eve party. In the story, the normal conditions of subverted anger and despondency on the reservation produce a metaphoric mini-hurricane sparked by fistfights, which turns into a mass brawl. Even as the fight worsens, nobody tries to stop it. Alexie criticizes the passive complacency of the onlookers.

> They were all witnesses and nothing more. For hundreds of years, Indians were witnesses to crimes of an epic scale. Victor's uncles were in the midst of a misdemeanor that would remain even if somebody was to die. One Indian killing another did not create a special kind of storm. This little kind of hurricane was generic. It didn't even deserve a name. (3)

In flashbacks, Alexie describes other little, personal hurricanes that wreaked havoc upon Victor (the protagonist), including a Christmas when Victor was five years old and his family didn't have any money for gifts, leading his father to cry in angry and furious desperation. Victor imagines "that his father's tears could have frozen solid in the severe reservation winters and shattered when they hit the floor. Sent millions of icy knives through the air, each specific and beautiful. Each dangerous and random" (5). The "little" hurricanes can also be internalized or repressed, such as when Victor's father drinks vodka on an empty stomach to distill his internalized hurricane of anger.

The little hurricane that Victor's uncles engender at the New Year's Eve party has a domino effect, forcing to the surface other repressed feelings of pain and rage in other Indians. Consequently, "the storm . . . moved from Indian to Indian at the party, giving each a specific, painful memory" (8). In the midst of the collective and individual fury, each Indian remembers an especially painful, personal experience of direct or indirect racism and/or wanton cruelty against them. Victor's father remembers when he and his father were spat upon by whites, and Victor's mother recalls how "the Indian Health Service doctor sterilized her moments after Victor was born." Here is where Alexie reveals how external, often racist acts or attitudes of non-Natives can produce internal, bottled-up rage that can lead to violence. Yet Alexie sees an ironic, positive by-product of this internalized rage and disillusion. The repressed animosity that produces these mini-hurricanes also forges strong bonds between family members on the reservation. While Alexie claims that this bond "is stronger than most anything," he also writes, "It's this same bond that causes so much pain." That is, being around other people who hold the same burdens of rage and disappointment reminds a person of what he or she individually carries. When a person remembers his or her individual pain, it causes a chain reaction of emerging anger amongst others, often culminating in huge, drunken fights. In fact, it appears that the pain outweighs the bond or that it's a bond of pain. In the night, Victor "listened for hours to every little hurricane spun from the larger hurricane that battered the reservation" (10). Fights break out in the snow outside, and Victor climbs back into bed with his drunk, passed-out parents. Even near his two parents, he realizes, "There was enough hunger in both, enough movement, enough geography and history, enough of everything to destroy the reservation and leave only random debris and broken furniture" (11). With this ending, Alexie suggests that ultimately Indians on the reservation are, in many ways, the greatest danger to themselves.

Apparent in the title is the main theme of another of Alexie's stories, "A Drug Called Tradition." In one manner, Alexie shows how, on the Spokane reservation (and presumably on other reservations as well), drugs, most prevalent among them alcohol, have replaced cultural traditions. At the same time, Alexie suggests that tradition itself is a kind of drug. This story takes place during the "second-largest party in reservation history" (12), which is hosted by Thomas Builds-the-Fire with money he received from the Washington Water Power company for allowing them to put power poles on his land. Unlike the tumultuous New Year's Eve party in "Every Little Hurricane," this party is more subdued, but it is still symptomatic of the despondency and near cultural bankruptcy on the reservation. Junior asks the narrator, Victor, if he has any hallucinogenic drugs, and although Victor doesn't have any, he "did have this brand new drug" (13). The three go out to Benjamin Lake to do a new drug, motivated by a desire to reclaim their cultural traditions, which they believe to involve visions. Victor tells Thomas, "We're going out to Benjamin Lake to do this new drug I got. It'll be very fucking Indian. Spiritual shit, you know?" (14). Even their so-called desire to reclaim their culture is misguided, derived from Western stereotypes of Indians, which dictate that "authentic" Indians have spiritual visions.

The drug, however, does not reconnect them with their culture nor provide them with any significant "visions." Rather, they have delusions of grandeur. In drug-induced pipe dreams, the drug allows them to see their unrealized potential or subverted culture. Victor dreams of Junior becoming an exceptional guitarist, while Junior dreams of stealing horses. Thomas, the most pragmatic of the three, realizes their misguided desires to try to reclaim their heritage: "They want to have their vision, to receive their true names, their adult names. That is the problem with Indians these days. They have the same names all their lives. Indians wear their names like a pair of bad shoes" (20). Thomas thus decries the loss of the traditional naming of Indians in childhood or adolescence according to personality, behavior, or action. The three stay out by the lake all night, but when they go back to the trading post, whatever they might have seen while on the chimera-producing drug eludes them. In the end, Thomas "threw away the rest of my new drug and hid in the backseat of Junior's car" (22). This is not to suggest that Indian culture or tradition has completely died out on the reservation, for the story ends with Big Mom, whom Alexie often uses in his stories and novels as the spiritual or matriarchal leader/gatekeeper of Indian culture, giving Thomas a traditional symbol of Indian culture: a drum. Even though the drum "was so small it could fit in the palm" of Thomas's hands, he believes that "if I played it a little, it might fill up the entire world" (23). Alexie thereby suggests that the smallest Indian cultural item or totem can be extraordinarily powerful in itself, surpassing any drug in its power.

Still, the atmosphere of the reservation is both intellectually and culturally confining to the point that Alexie, in one story, compares it to a prison. In *The Business of Fancydancing,* Alexie wrote a story about Thomas Builds-the-Fire learning to use his imagination when trouble and mayhem break the monotony of reservation life and he holds the reservation postmistress hostage with the idea of a gun. The Kafka-inspired "The Trial of Thomas Builds-the-Fire" is a continuation of that story in which Thomas is kept prisoner in a tribal cell because of his previous actions and because he "had also threatened to make significant changes in the tribal vision" (93). Thomas is set free only when he agrees to keep silent; however, Alexie casts an accusatory finger at the powers that be, either white people heading the BIA or stooges like tribal police officer/chairman David WalksAlong, as wanting to uphold the status quo, thereby keeping Indians on the reservation deprived of hope or imagination, virtually enslaved. This story takes place after twenty years of Thomas's silence, when he starts making noises, forming "syllables that contained more emotion and meaning than entire sentences constructed by the BIA. A noise that sounded something like *rain* had given Esther courage to leave her husband, tribal chairman David Walks-Along" (94). Once again, Alexie suggests that a small individual action can have monumental aftereffects, causing a ripple effect on the reservation and helping to forge change. David Walks-Along appears to realize this and subsequently arrests Thomas, perceiving him as a threat, a would-be leader of the reservation who could help awaken Spokane Indians from their communal daze, a state in which the BIA can keep them powerless.

Thomas finally begins talking during his trial, but like Joseph K. in Kafka's *The Trial,* Thomas is not informed of the charges brought against him. While defending himself, Thomas attempts to reclaim Indian history, decries its usurpation by contemporary whites, and tells stories of atrocities committed against Indians by European settlers. However, his attempt proves to be in vain, as the story ends with a declaration that Thomas was sentenced to "two concurrent life terms in the Walla Walla State Penitentiary" (102). Telling these stories, Alexie suggests, is dangerous because they upset commonly held notions of American history, in addition to forcing to the surface repressed anger in Indians. Still, even imprisonment cannot defeat Thomas, who continues telling stories in a bus that takes him to prison, which he calls "a new kind of reservation" (103). Even though he is to be imprisoned, Alexie suggests, his imagination and creative facilities cannot ultimately be caged.

Thomas reappears in other stories, including "This Is What It Means to Say Phoenix, Arizona," a story that would become the blueprint for Alexie's film *Smoke Signals*. This story focuses on Victor who, after losing his job, discovers that his father has died in Phoenix and plans to go there to claim his meager inheritance. Victor gets only a hundred dollars from the tribal council and enlists Thomas's help. Once again, in this story and through the character of Thomas, Alexie demonstrates how people with imaginative abilities and tendencies are typically ostracized on the reservation, in an exact antithesis of traditional Indian cultures, which typically revere imagination and the storyteller. While Thomas is the resident storyteller, he is also the resident pariah "because he told the same damn stories over and over again" (62). Thomas has mystical tendencies, which lead him to jump off the roof of the tribal school because he thought he could fly. Even though Thomas broke his leg, the other Indians "hated Thomas for his courage, his brief moment as a bird" because "one of his dreams came true for just a second, just enough to make it real" (70–71). Victor represents more of what Alexie perceives as a typical contemporary Indian, whereas Thomas is closer to what Alexie believes a contemporary Indian should be like (although Thomas's stories can at times be banal and his actions occasionally misguided). Telling stories allows Thomas to maintain Indian heritage and culture, both of which Victor doesn't care about until Thomas's act of kindness, which helps change Victor psychologically. Consequently, after returning to the reservation, "Victor was ashamed of himself. Whatever happened to the tribal ties, the sense of community? The only real thing he shared with anybody was a bottle and broken dreams. He owed Thomas something, anything" (74). At the end of the story, Victor agrees to listen to one of Thomas's stories, which marks a connection forged between two individuals, showing that Alexie does not believe that community on the reservation or traditional Indian culture has disintegrated beyond repair.

Storytelling runs in the Builds-the-Fire family, as evidenced by the story "A Train Is an Order of Occurrence Designed to Lead to Some Result," which focuses on Thomas's grandfather, Samuel Builds-the-Fire, who works as a maid in a hotel. The story takes place on Samuel's birthday. Samuel is isolated and distant from his family. Despite the fact that, like his grandson, Samuel is creative and imaginative, a natural-born cultural leader who "could pick the pieces of a story from the street and change the world for a few moments" (132), he, like Thomas, has become an outcast, a symbol of the spiritual deterioration of the reservation and of Indian people in general: "Samuel lived on the reservation, alone, for as long as he could, without money or company. All his friends had died and all the younger people on the reservation had no time for stories" (135). The isolation proves unbearable after Samuel loses his job as a maid, a menial position but one that he does with commitment and skill. The loss of his job leads the previously abstaining Samuel to visit a bar for the first time in his life. After his first drink ever, Samuel thinks that he comes to an epiphany, but he doesn't realize that it's a misguided epiphany, the same misguided epiphany, Alexie suggests, that most alcoholic Indians come to: "With each glass of beer, Samuel gained a few ounces of wisdom, courage. But after a while, he began to understand too much about fear and failure, too" (134). To some extent, Alexie criticizes Samuel's and Thomas's romantic naïveté, for their desire to tell stories does neither any good. However, it is not entirely their fault: they have no real audience anymore since stories have lost their mystical, personal, and cultural appeal to other Indians. The story ends with a drunken Samuel falling on train tracks as a train approaches, beaten down by the world and drunkenness, having lost his place in the world. While it is not clear if he will be hit by a train, Alexie does not sugarcoat the ending, leaving the reader with the idea that there are many Indians like Samuel, who selflessly want to improve the conditions on the reservation but are ultimately unsuccessful, casualties of mass apathy and despondency.

The outlook is not particularly brighter when Alexie considers the intersection points between the Indian and white worlds. Whereas in *First Indian on the Moon* he examined the transformative possibilities of interracial romance for improving Indian-white relations, in the title story, "The Lone Ranger and Tonto Fistfight in Heaven," there is little hope of bridging what Alexie here portrays as a chasm between the two ethnicities, cultures, and modes of life. The story begins in urban Seattle. Having trouble sleeping, the narrator goes to a 7-Eleven. That the narrator has worked for a Seattle 7-Eleven is important in the sense that it should make him feel more empathy for the graveyard-shift worker, but instead, they play a cat-and-mouse game with each other. On one level, their encounter is the fight described in the title of the story, a subtle battle for dominance, which, Alexie suggests, exists on a daily basis between Natives and non-Natives and possibly between other minorities and the white mainstream. Generally uninterested in the graveyard-shift worker, the narrator generalizes that he "looked like they all do. Acne scars and a bad haircut, work pants that showed off his white socks, and those cheap black shoes that have no-support" (181).

The narrator believes that the white cashier scrutinizes him because of his color and thereby perceives him as a threat. Furthermore, he connects this feeling and the uneasy encounter between himself and the graveyard-shift worker with the turbulent relationship he had with a white woman, explaining that she told him, "I started to look at her that way, too" (182). The narrator and the white woman are also stand-ins for the Lone Ranger and Tonto. Their tumultuous relationship motivates the narrator to obtain a graveyard-shift position so that he could "spend as much time away from her possible" (182). However, the narrator does not leave her at this point; rather, he thrives upon conflict and rage, which relates to the title of the story in the sense that in the narrator's conception of heaven or of an ideal world, there is fighting or conflict. The narrator believes either that conflict is impossible to avoid or that it is part of his ideal conception of the world.

At the same time, a good deal of that conflict and anger stems from the narrator's feelings of exclusion and/or displacement as a reservation Indian living in a city (Seattle), which exacerbates everyday battles that the narrator has to wage against others, normally whites. He drives around Seattle, "searching for something familiar," only to end up in an upscale residential neighborhood where a police officer stops him and tells him: "You're making people nervous. You don't fit the profile of the neighborhood" (183). Once again, a major conflict develops between the narrator and somebody else, in this case, a person in a position of power. The speaker thinks, "I wanted to tell him that I didn't really fit the profile of the country but I knew it would just get me into trouble" (183). For the narrator, who feels largely excluded from mainstream America, most encounters with whites are fraught with tension and are ultimately demeaning. Conflict, therefore, catalyzes the narrator's struggle to achieve a perceived sense of equality.

This perspective affects the narrator to the extent that if conflict doesn't immediately exist, he often creates it. The speaker taunts the white 7-Eleven worker, telling him he's just getting a Creamsicle, admitting it's a "sick twist to pull on the guy, but it was late and I was bored" (183). He even admits that "I wanted to whistle low and menacingly but I never learned to whistle." Even though, up close, he recognizes that the white clerk was "just misplaced and marked by loneliness," he continues to taunt him, probably because the narrator believes that by mere dint of his ethnicity, the clerk has power over the narrator. The narrator continues his struggle for power by asking for a Cherry Slushie and then toying with the clerk when he asks him what size. In part wanting the clerk to feel threatened by his aberrant behavior, the narrator tells him to forget the Slushie, and asks him if he knows the words to the theme of *The Brady Bunch,* which makes the employee laugh. To some extent, this is also the work of the narrator, who defuses the situation and makes a truce with the clerk. The white man tells him to take the

Creamsicle for free because, as the speaker concludes, "He was the graveyard-shift manager and those little demonstrations of power tickled him" (184). What the narrator doesn't admit or realize, however, is that he is also involved in a struggle for power with the graveyard-shift worker and previously with his white ex-girlfriend, frequently breaking lamps to overexaggerate their arguments or to bring a sense of physical drama to their verbal arguments. His intrinsically combative nature comes through in the comment, "I walked through that relationship with an executioner's hood. Or more appropriately, with war paint and sharp arrows" (185).

The narrator's conception that conflict, often violent, is at the heart of Indian-white relationships becomes even clearer when he relates a violent and sexual dream in which he and his white girlfriend are found in flagrante delicto, which sparks a full-fledged war between whites and Indians. The most vivid image of the narrator's dream is that of "three mounted soldiers play[ing] polo with a dead Indian woman's head. When I first dreamed it, I thought it was just a product of my anger and imagination. But since then, I've read similar accounts of that kind of evil in the old West. Even more terrifying, though, is the fact that those kinds of brutal things are happening today in places like El Salvador" (186). The narrator emphasizes this part of his dream because he wants the reader to believe that there hasn't been much cultural progression and that the possibility of such atrocities occurring again, even to a lesser degree, aren't that remote. That he leaves his white girlfriend after this dream indicates the extent to which he has given up the effort to bridge the gap between the Indian and white world, which, the story suggests, is inherently fraught with violence and disaster.

When his fight for power with the 7-Eleven worker reaches a stalemate, the narrator tries to up the ante by acting unruly. After finishing the Creamsicle, he purposely creates a scene by shouting loudly, which startles nearby residents and brings the police. When the police drive by, the narrator mockingly waves at them. The narrator notes that the police "waved back accidentally" (187), presumably because they were expecting a less than friendly gesture on the part of the narrator. This is yet another struggle for power between the narrator and the police, who, the narrator made clear earlier, regard him as somewhat of a menace. Presumably, the narrator feels that he has won this conflict by confounding the expectations of the police officers. Furthermore, the narrator reads the newspapers and finds more incidents of violence seemingly everywhere, or at least he is drawn to the parts of the paper that display violence, civil war, terrorist bombings, and plane crashes, all of which help fuel his perception of the world as primarily violent and conflicted.

Another struggle for power occurs when the narrator goes back to the reservation and just watches television for weeks, avoiding getting a job. Here, conflicts arise within the reservation and between the narrator and his family. A lack of ambition would have been fine for other Indians, the narrator suggests, "But I was special, a former college student, a smart kid. I was one of those Indians who was supposed to make it, to rise above the rest of the reservation like a fucking eagle or something. I was a new kind of warrior" (188). The conflicts become offset when he plays basketball, which serves as an outlet for his anger and rage, calming him to the point that he begins searching for employment and gets a job in Spokane as a clerk in a high school. A few months later, when his white ex-girlfriend calls him up, she tells him she wants "to change the world" (190), but the narrator has no response to that, possibly because he doesn't think the world can be changed or because he doesn't feel he has any agency. Rather, he continues to be unable to find balance, evidenced by his continuing insomnia, but he still reaches a strange peace in his unsettled state: "It may take hours, even years, for me to sleep again. There's nothing surprising or disappointing in that. I know how all my dreams end anyway" (190).

One problem is that the speaker doesn't have a stable family life and identity, and Alexie suggests that familial or communal stability can offset the perpetual conflicts that Indians endure, especially when living in predominantly white-dominated areas. This is apparent in the story "Family Portrait," which decries the pervasive, deteriorating influence of television upon family life. The story begins: "The television was always loud, too loud, until every conversation was distorted, fragmented. 'Dinner' sounded like 'Leave me alone.' 'I love you' sounded like 'Inertia.' 'Please' sounded like 'Sacrifice'" (191). While trying to recall his familial life, the speaker notes: "I don't know where all the years went. I remember only the television in detail. All the other moments worth remembering became stories that changed with each telling, until nothing was aboriginal or recognizable" (192). Television helps mutate his memories, leading him to think of "real life" as in flux and changeable. In a way, it effaces the divisions between fantasy and reality. The speaker describes how "in the summer of 1972 or 1973 or only in our minds, the reservation disappeared." However positive that might appear on the surface, it only serves to divert them from reality. As a result, they ignore their plight and do nothing to try to ameliorate their living and spiritual conditions. In this story, popular culture—more specifically, television—serves as a drug, creating distances between people, drowning out all other voices and identities, and encouraging lethargy: "The television was always loud, too loud, until every emotion was measured by the half hour. We hid our faces behind masks that suggested other histories" (198). Alexie ends this family portrait with no real solution but with the aftereffects of the pervasive influence of television: "We stared across the room at each other, waited for the conversation and the conversion" (198).

Not all of Alexie's stories are despondent accounts of characters virtually defeated by poverty and hopelessness on the reservation. "Somebody Kept Saying Powwow" concerns Norma, "a cultural lifeguard" of the reservation, "watching out for those of us that were so close to drowning" (199). Norma tells Junior, the narrator, that "Indians are the most sensitive people on the planet. For that matter, Indians are more sensitive than animals, too. We don't just watch things happen. Watching automatically makes the watcher part of the happening. That's what Norma taught me" (200). Norma tells Junior this not because she necessarily believes it (nor does Alexie necessarily believe it) but because it counteracts internalized feelings of low self-worth. Still, the narrator uses Norma as a role model for the reservation: "Norma lived her life like we should all do. She didn't drink or smoke. But she could spend a night in the Powwow Tavern and dance hard. She could dance Indian or white. And that's a mean feat, since the two methods of dancing are mutually exclusive." Norma is also "a rodeo queen," a "roper, a breaker of wild ponies" (202), and is sexually promiscuous, but she also devotes herself to other poverty-stricken and drug-abusing Indians on the reservation. Since Indian reservations, as Alexie portrays them, tend to be male-dominated, Norma, as a female heroine, also breaks a cultural mold.

Similarly, Alexie aims to upset stereotypes in the humorous story "Because My Father Always Said He Was the Only Indian Who Saw Jimi Hendrix Play 'The Star-Spangled Banner' at Woodstock." This story concerns the speaker's father, an Indian and an antiwar demonstrator during the late 1960s. "During the sixties," Alexie begins, "my father was a perfect hippie since all hippies were trying to be Indians. Because of that, how could anyone recognize that my father was trying to make a social statement" (24). With this, Alexie shows how Indians were, in a way, excluded from mainstream existence during the 1960s, not allowed to be part of the countercultural movement, which, in many ways, mirrored the culture of a ethnic group they purposely or inadvertently excluded. Even when the narrator's father protests the war, literally fighting against National Guardsmen, his actions are appropriated by the media, who photographs him with the caption: "ONE WARRIOR AGAINST WAR AND PEACEFUL GATHERING TURNS INTO NATIVE UPRISING" (25). The narrator's father, of course, is not a warrior, but the photographer capitalizes and eventually profits from the stereotype of Indian men as warriors, and the photo goes on to win a Pulitzer. This story also demonstrates a generation gap between the narrator's father and the narrator, who is envious of his father and his experiences. The narrator complains that his generation doesn't have an opportunity to fight in a war like his father's generation did. The narrator's father refutes his son's desire by stating, "Why the hell would you want to fight a war for this country? It's been trying to kill Indians since the very beginning. Indians are pretty much born soldiers anyway. Don't need a uniform to prove it" (29). As the story progresses, it becomes less clear whether the speaker's father ever attended Woodstock or, for that matter, whether any of his stories are true.

Alexie undertakes the project of charting the effects of the white world upon Indians and provides an account of a typical reservation childhood in "Indian Education," an autobiographical account of a reservation boy's (possibly Alexie's) schooling. Year by year, this never-named male child must deal with taunts and violence from both non-Natives and Natives. The story is segmented into short entries for grades one through twelve. During first grade, the speaker is continually beat up by other Indian students because his glasses and bad haircut make him an easy target, until he finally fights back. With his characteristic humor, Alexie describes the cruelty of the other kids: "I was always falling down; my Indian name was Junior Falls Down. Sometimes it was Bloody Nose or Steal-His-Lunch. Once, it was Cries-Like-a-White-Boy, even though none of us had seen a white boy cry" (172). Conflict then, is not purely an aftereffect of interactions with whites. To a large extent, it is a by-product of the reservation, where violence is prevalent even in early childhood. The narrator also experiences racism for the first time in the second grade from a teacher he mocks, who retaliates by making him eat a spelling test. Subsequently, the teacher writes the narrator's parents and tells them "to either cut my braids or keep me home from class" (173). When the narrator's parents confront the teacher, the teacher condescendingly mutters, "indians, indians, indians." The narrator emphasizes that "she said it without capitalization."

By the time he enters sixth grade, the narrator witnesses a fight and learns "the most valuable lesson about living in the white world: *Always throw the first punch*" (176, italics in original). In seventh grade, he kisses a white girl and by doing so "felt the good-byes I was saying to my entire tribe" (176). Even at this early age, the narrator has developed a strong ethnic identity. In the bathroom in the eighth grade, he overhears white girls' "nervous whispers of anorexia and bulimia," and he "sat back and watched them grow skinny from self-pity" (177). He compares their plight to that of Indians on his reservation who have to eat commodity food, such as "canned beef that even the dogs wouldn't eat. But we ate it day after day and grew skinny from self-pity. There is more than one way to starve." These realizations incite jealousy and anger toward the white world in him. In tenth grade, the speaker passes his driving test on the same day another Indian commits suicide in a car. When asked why he did it by a white state trooper, the Indians, including the precocious narrator, say they don't know, "but when we look in the mirror, see the history of our tribe in our eyes, taste failure in the tap water, and shake with old tears, we understand completely. Believe me, everything looks like a noose if you stare at it long enough" (178). In eleventh grade, he loses a basketball game for a mostly white school, whose team calls themselves the "Indians," even though the speaker is "probably the only actual Indian ever to play for a team with such a mascot. This morning I pick up the sports page and read the headline: INDIANS LOSE AGAIN. Go ahead and tell me none of this is supposed to hurt me very much" (179). In twelfth grade, the speaker is named valedictorian of his high school. In the postscript about a class reunion, Victor wonders why they should have one when they have "a reunion every weekend at the Powwow Tavern" (180). With this ending, Alexie suggests that "Indian education" is often wasted and that, in a way, it's less an intellectual education than an indoctrination into racism, sadness, and despondency; what little education they receive is often frittered away after graduation.

However, one activity that Alexie believes to have transformative power in counteracting the despondency and grief on the reservation and forming community is athletics, specifically basketball. Alan Velie explains the importance of basketball on the reservation:

> More than most ethnic groups, Indians have a strong sense of history; they think constantly of their glamorous past of mounted warfare. They are painfully aware that the days of stealing horses and making war are over, but they are not sure what to replace those activities with. The chief substitute is basketball, a game that reservation Indians love as much as urban blacks do. Unfortunately, whereas blacks commonly use sports as a way out of the ghetto, Indians, though they are often as gifted, are so tied to tribal life that it is extremely rare for them to make it to college as athletes or scholars.[6]

The story "The Only Traffic Signal on the Reservation Doesn't Flash Red Anymore" concerns Julius Windmaker, a reservation basketball hero. The narrator, a former basketball star himself, thinks he understands Julius: "I still felt that ache in my bones, that need to be better than everyone else. It's that need to be the best, that feeling of immortality that drives a ballplayer. And when it disappears, for whatever reason, that ballplayer is never the same person, on or off the court" (46). The narrator's glory days have disappeared, suggesting the question of to what extent Alexie truly believes in the power of athletics, since athletic glory is normally fleeting at best. Still, the narrator defends the importance of the athletic hero on the reservation: "In the outside world, a person can be a hero one second and a nobody the next . . . but a reservation hero is remembered. A reservation hero is a hero forever. In fact, their status grows over the years as the stories are told and retold" (48). However, this reservation hero, Julius, fritters his abilities away as he takes to drinking. Although "Indians kind of see ballplayers as saviors" (52), the story concludes on a sarcastic note with the narrator and his friend pinning their hopes on a third-grade basketball player, Lucy, who plays on the sixth-grade boys team. While it is hardly possible that any one athlete will change the plight of Indians, it does provide hope.

There are two other ways in which Alexie believes that the reservation can be empowered: through the imagination and through humor. In "Imagining the Reservation," Alexie offers hypothetical rewrites of history or imagined occurrences in order to inspire the imagination and transcend the present:

> Imagine Crazy Horse invented the atom bomb in 1876 and detonated it over Washington, D.C. Would the urban Indians still be sprawled around the one-room apartment in the cable television reservation? Imagine a loaf of bread could feed the entire tribe. Didn't you know Jesus Christ was a Spokane Indian? Imagine Columbus landed in 1492 and some tribe or another drowned him in the ocean. Would Lester FallsApart still be shoplifting in the 7-11? (149–50)

Whereas Alexie insisted in his previous collection that Poetry = Anger × Imagination, in this collection Alexie insists that "Survival = Anger × Imagination. Imagination is the only weapon on the reservation" (150). For Alexie, then, poetry and survival have become basically synonymous. Poetry is an act of survival; it represents life and opposes death. As proof of the power of the imagination, Alexie recalls the story of a hobo who froze to death in a refrigerator that wasn't plugged in but, believing it was, still froze. Addressing the reader, Alexie writes:

What do you believe in? Does every Indian depend on Hollywood for a twentieth-century vision? Listen: when I was young, living on the reservation, I imagined the potatoes grew larger, filled my stomach, reversed the emptiness . . . my father and I telling stories about the food we wanted the most. We imagined oranges, Pepsi-Cola, chocolate, deer jerky. We imagined the salt on our skin could change the world. (151)

Yet the narrator, presumably Alexie, struggles with how Indians can be empowered when the very language they use is that of the colonizers, hence keeping them enslaved. "How can we imagine a new language," Alexie writes, "when the language of the enemy keeps our dismembered tongues tied to his belt? How can we imagine a new alphabet when the old jumps off billboards down into our stomachs? . . . How do we imagine a new life when a pocketful of quarters weighs our possibilities down?" (152).

If the imagination cannot salvage Indian lives on its own, humor, Alexie suggests, may also work, but it can be a double-edged sword. "The Approximate Size of My Favorite Tumor" shows both the transformative and destructive possibilities for humor as both life-affirming and negating. The story concerns a man, Jimmy One-Horse or Many Horses, who cannot stop telling jokes, even after he is diagnosed with cancer. His wife becomes increasingly upset at him because of his continual joking about his illness. Despite the fact that humor hastens their marriage's deterioration, Jimmy contemplates: "Still, you have to realize that laughter saved Norma and me from pain, too. Humor was an antiseptic that cleaned the deepest of personal wounds" (164). Still, Jimmy's rationalization is not enough to keep Norma with him, although she does return to him after several months. She tells him she came back because the man she was living with was too serious. "And maybe," she said, "because making fry bread and helping people die are the two last things Indians are good at." The story concludes with Jimmy's humorous retort: "'Well,' I said, 'At least you're good at one of them.' And we laughed" (170). Humor thereby ameliorates devastating situations and makes poverty and despondency bearable. It is a tool that Alexie uses frequently in his writings. Ultimately, Alexie suggests, humor—along with creativity and athletics—can help restore pride in self, culture, and community in Indian reservations.

CHAPTER 4

Reservation Blues

In an interview conducted by Tomson Highway, Sherman Alexie explains the genesis of his first novel, *Reservation Blues* (1995): "I had a two-book deal with Atlantic Monthly Press. I had a one-sentence description of a novel: it was an all-Indian Catholic rock-and-roll band."[1] Presumably, the idea was intriguing enough to Atlantic Monthly since they quickly approved the project. Indeed, books written about music, specifically pop music, have a greater chance of reaching a larger audience because music transcends boundaries. By this time, Alexie did have a repertoire of characters that he used repeatedly in his first three collections, which he decided to use and modify in *Reservation Blues*. Alexie describes *Reservation Blues* as a "sequel because many of the same characters and situations that existed in *The Lone Ranger and Tonto Fistfight in Heaven* are in it. It's set on my reservation with three main characters: Thomas Builds-the-Fire, a misfit storyteller of the Spokane tribe, Victor Joseph, an alcoholic angry Indian guy, and Junior Polatkin, the happy-go-lucky failure."[2] This supports the idea that one of Alexie's purposes is to construct a Faulkner-like microcosmic space through which to investigate larger social, cultural, and psychological issues. By placing traditional African American music and contemporary rock music in the contemporary context of the reservation and then having individuals from the reservation move into mainstream white America, *Reservation Blues* straddles the lines between ethnicities, cultures, time frames, religions, gender perspectives, and literary genres. It is a realistic novel providing an in-depth look at reservation life, but it is also a magic-realist work replete with seemingly immortal, ghostly musicians like Robert Johnson and with deceased American soldiers from the nineteenth century in the guise of corporate music executives. In this novel, a guitar can talk and popular American musicians and icons like Elvis and Janis Joplin have been taught by a possibly immortal Spokane Indian named Big Mom, the unacknowledged matriarchal leader of the Spokane tribe. Alexie toys with Indian creation myths and forges alliances while uncovering mass conflict and antagonism between African, white, and Native cultures.

In the first part of the novel, Alexie provides a familiar, despondent portrait of the Spokane Indian Reservation. The monotonous, virtually self-enclosed hermetic environment has become, in a way, a casualty of its own homogeneity. Since its establishment in 1881, there has not been a single visitor to the Spokane Indian Reservation. Alexie portrays Thomas Builds-the-Fire in a similar manner as in his previous stories, but this time he places greater emphasis on Thomas's outsider status. In the topsy-turvy, upside-down environment of the reservation, Thomas has become a virtual leper instead of one of the tribe's leaders, a position traditionally reserved for the residential storyteller, which, in reality, is Thomas's thankless role. Furthermore, Indians on the reservation have been led astray by American popular images of bellicose male Indian warriors as the epitome of masculinity, a virtually unrealizable standard that often leads men to despondency and drug abuse. Later in the novel, Checkers, a Flathead who joins the all-Indian rock group Coyote Springs, asserts that one of the main contributing factors for the desperation and impoverishment of the reservation is the (predominantly male) "need to be superhuman in the poverty of a reservation."³ While Checkers criticizes the arrogant machismo of these Indians, most Indian women are not like her and buy into the desired codes for male authenticity as warrior figures. Thomas, who doesn't fit the mold, becomes romantically and social isolated on the reservation. Like Thomas, Junior, a former college student turned water-truck driver, has been duped by media stereotypes into thinking that, as an Indian, he should have mystical and instructional visions. The third major character, Victor, more closely adheres to the codes for male authenticity, being more of the reservation strongman/bully, but he too appears to be somewhat of a puppet of mainstream American popular culture, more image than substance, given his propensity to dress in disco-era clothing.

Alexie emphasizes how Thomas has, in a way, become an outcast because of his attempt to uphold tribal culture in a reservation that has lost interest in its own culture and history, emphasizing that Thomas is the only Indian on the reservation who tries to maintain Spokane cultural traditions, while everyone else has forgotten or neglected them. However, Alexie does not entirely blame the Spokanes. Rather, through Thomas's satirical "The Reservation's Ten Commandments as Given by the United States of America to the Spokane Indians," Alexie exposes what he believes to be the hidden truth behind the American government's policies toward Indians, which includes, "You shall not make for yourself an independent and self-sufficient government, for I am a jealous bureaucracy" (154).

Furthermore, the ghettolike environment of the reservation, with its monotonous, decrepit HUD housing, few paltry stores, and mass unemployment, an environment inhabited largely by "dreams that were murdered" (23) in a way resembles the small, sharecropping communities of the South in the early twentieth century, which were intrinsically a catalyst for the development of blues music (especially Delta blues). One reservation resident, The Man-who-was-probably-Lakota, captures the bleak atmosphere with his daily mantra, "The end of the world is near," a fair representation of the unconscious desires of many of the hopeless, despondent residents, including Thomas's perpetually drunk father, whom Thomas frequently finds passed out in front of his house. Furthermore, most Indians subsist upon the meager, unhealthy supplies provided by the reservation trading post, such as Diet Pepsi, Spam, and Wonder bread, which further contribute to the impoverished atmosphere.

The bleak residents of the reservations sometimes resort to violence, as evidenced by Victor, an adult bully who frequently picks on smaller, weaker Indians like Thomas, with help from Junior, Victor's frequent accomplice on his violent rampages. Victor's and to a lesser extent Junior's violent behavior are manifestations of thwarted bitterness, rage, and powerlessness. In a culture that champions fierce and bellicose masculinity, men who cannot or do not fit the mold—which would include virtually all men on the reservation—are left in a particularly precarious position. They begin fighting with each other to take out their aggression and frustration at their overall powerlessness and poverty. Like caged animals, they are driven to establish a futile pecking order, with the stronger Indians like Victor preying on the weaker ones like Thomas. Representative of most on the reservation, Victor has become singularly consumed with the pursuit of money while Junior has settled into a seemingly comfortable routine of eating, working, and sleeping with only vague, amorphous material desires. Only Thomas has any larger social, cultural, and spiritual concerns, evident in his allegorical stories about the reservation, such as one about turtles that live in "caverns beneath the reservation and feed on failed dreams" (27). As Bobby Lake-Thom explains, "Turtles of all kinds, both water and land Turtles, are good signs and very good powers. The Turtle is considered very sacred to most Native American tribal cultures. The Turtle is a healer and protector. It can grant long life, wisdom, and good health."[4] If a turtle feeds on failed dreams, then the sacred has become desecrated and/or profane, and the turtle can provide none of what it is traditionally thought to provide. Along similar lines, Thomas decries a rampant nihilism, concluding that "nobody believed in anything on the reservation" (28).

Furthermore, Alexie makes a connection between television as exacerbating desire and passivity as well as confusing identity and increasing feelings of inferiority. Not only does television constantly remind Thomas of his poverty, it helps make him aware of the discrepancy between the lives of mainstream American whites and Indians and also literally infects his dreams. Alexie writes that Thomas "dreamed of television and hunger" because, for Thomas and most Indians, the two have become intertwined (70). Television exacerbates hunger at the same time that it further isolates Thomas, an Indian, from the media landscape that is dominated by white actors and actresses. Instead of seeking it in the reservation that has rejected him, Thomas seeks community when he watches television, but when he does find Indians on television, they are either portrayed in a stereotypical fashion as savages or mercilessly massacred by settlers/cowboys. For instance, in one particular program Thomas watches, cowboys tell the bellicose, savage Indians that they've come in friendship, but they end up electrocuting Indians, which for Thomas—and possibly for Alexie as well—illustrates the shaky ground upon which Indian-white relations stand.

Indian-white relations are not helped any by the decrepit conditions on the reservation. Although Alexie does cast a good deal of the blame upon the environment, he does not vilify it. The land itself is still their home, a part of their heritage and culture, despite the broken-down economic and spiritual conditions. Alexie emphasizes that the reservation still possesses "power," "magic," and "joys" (96). Indeed, Thomas frequently personifies the reservation by saying hello to the night sky and calling the crickets "father." Yet the actual reservation is more of a repository of the living dead, many of whom are severe alcoholics. Checkers calls these perpetually drunk, seemingly vacuous individuals, "Indian zombies." Indeed, Alexie makes the point that not only do "all Indians grow up with drunks" but also that all the major characters in *Reservation Blues* "had run from drunks" (151). In part, Alexie implicates mainstream popular culture for helping foster the stereotypical image of the "philosophizing," drunk Indian, when, in reality, "most Indians never drink" but nobody ever notices them. Still, Alexie blames most Indians on the reservation for glorifying sentimental and kindly alcoholics. At the same time, Alexie uncovers a solidarity amongst Indians, even of differing tribes, noting the close-knit network of reservations composed of Indians each of whom could be "a potential lover, friend, or relative." At the same time, Alexie portrays the typical hierarchy on the reservation: those at the administrative top, who possess the most power, tend to be the least ethnically Indian and cruelly wield their power over others like tribal police officer Wilson, who dubiously claims a modicum of Indian ancestry through a distant relative but has no real compassion or interest in the welfare of his "fellow" Indians.

Still, in *Reservation Blues,* Alexie aims not only to revive Native culture and traditions but also to find productive intersecting points between Native and other cultures. Most important, with his use of blues music in the novel, Alexie makes connections and parallels between African American and Native American culture and traditions. As Peter Aschoff argues, "The blues is, first and foremost, an oral act and a performance ritual."[5] Likewise, Native American traditions and culture are primarily oral. Traditionally, Native American music, though extraordinarily powerful in its own right, is primarily instrumental, performative, and drum-based, without as much emphasis placed upon the lyrics, which are central to the blues. Ralph Ellison has described the blues as "one of the techniques through which Negroes have survived and kept their courage during the long period when many whites assumed, as some still assume, that they were afraid."[6] Similarly, Alexie sees the blues as offering empowerment and transformation. It is an expansive music that, as Aschoff argues, honors freedom and encourages the mind to think beyond the borders of the reservation.

During the early years of the blues, many people thought of it as being the devil's music or associated it with satanic rituals or worship, but, as Peter Aschoff points out, that is only if you interpret the blues from Western paradigms. Most African and Native American religions believe in the existence and manifestations of ghosts or spirits.[7] Furthermore, the blues forces individuals to accept human weakness and vulnerability, realizations that Alexie believes to be crucial in improving conditions on the reservation, because they can counteract the oppressive patriarchal system that sets impossible archetypes for men as omnipotent warriors while marginalizing the women. Furthermore, as Jon Spencer argues, the blues champions what he calls the "badman" character, someone not quite as evil as his name suggests, but one who could counteract oppression, "a synthesis of traits of the trickster and conjurer traditions, which were African religious retentions among the enslaved communities."[8] This would be an appropriate new hero for the reservation, and in many ways, it is also Alexie's personal objective as a writer.

Onto the Spokane Reservation stumbles a quintessential "badman" character, legendary blues guitarist Robert Johnson who, according to myth, sold his soul to the devil in order to become a guitar virtuoso. While history tells us that Johnson was murdered by either an ex-girlfriend or jealous husband when he was twenty-seven, in *Reservation Blues* Alexie envisions him as a restless spirit, seemingly doomed to wander the planet, never able to find personal contentment or even a stable home until the time of the present narrative. Johnson's initial appearance on the reservation is important in that it demonstrates the extreme passivity and general hopelessness of people living on the reservation. Even though "the entire reservation knew about the black man five minutes after he showed up at the crossroads" (3), no one has the courage to talk with him except Thomas. While other Indians watch the two of them, Alexie emphasizes that only Thomas takes a genuine interest by approaching and welcoming Johnson. One perceptive critic, Karen Jorgensen, argues that Alexie uses Johnson as a doppelgänger of Thomas to expose "correlations between characters where none would ordinarily be apparent."[9] Furthermore, "as the New Testament indicates," she writes, "the name Thomas means 'twin,' and although they are Indian and non-Indian, Thomas and Robert are 'twins': they are both creators, storytellers with words and music, who have an inherent need to tell their stories."[10] In support of her theory, when Johnson says he's caught some sickness, Alexie writes that Thomas likewise knows about sickness, and both are mentally and physically bent or hunched because of the burdens they carry. Alexie indicates that, through his stories, Thomas wishes to find a new form with which to transform the dismal conditions of the reservation and possibly to provide hope and transcendence to those living on the reservation. Unfortunately, the entire reservation ignores his stories. He finds a new healing form in the blues, which adds power and importance to his words.

In *Reservation Blues,* Alexie reclaims or appropriates music —more specifically, the blues—for the Spokane Indian Reservation, but his conception of music is more multidimensional in comparison to traditional Western conceptions. In the novel, horses can sing and were taught by Big Mom. Alexie's creation myth considers the blues to be a natural, indigenous American music/force, originating from animals like horses who reacted with apprehension and terror to the cruel, destructive ways of white settlers. Alexie writes that when Europeans settled the country and subsequently abused the land, the people, and the animals, specifically, the horses "sounded so pained and tortured that Big Mom could never have imagined it before the white men came" (9). The blues then originates with the colonization of the land and its people. However, Alexie does not show Natives to have been completely colonized. With Big Mom, Alexie creates a character/entity stronger than any colonizer. In part, Big Mom symbolically represents the immortal spirit of the Spokane Reservation, as she's been there for over a hundred years and has purportedly taught all her horses to sing. In a magic-realist mode, Alexie makes Big Mom the musical teacher and inspiration for noted mainstream musicians and singers such as Janis Joplin, Jimi Hendrix, and Marvin Gaye. In other words, Big Mom sees these musicians as part of a musical ethos that resulted from the settling of the country and continues through the continuing pain and dislocation of oppressed minority groups. Johnson's guitar, which feeds on despondency and desperation, finds a perfect owner/servant in Thomas Builds-the-Fire.

Significantly, the next reincarnation of Big Mom's horses comes out of the reservation, not from the outside world. Johnson gives his guitar to Thomas, and, surprisingly, the guitar has its own identity and is able to talk. It is significant that Johnson is able to leave his guitar with Thomas because, until then, Johnson was held captive by the guitar and could not leave it with anyone. Johnson passing his guitar to Thomas is a symbolic exchange between the African American and Native American community. Alexie suggests that the contemporary reservation mirrors late-nineteenth-century/early-twentieth-century impoverished African American communities. The guitar tells Thomas that "the blues always make us remember" (23), which is, in a sense, what Alexie wants to accomplish. He wants the blues to reawaken Indian culture and traditions, just as it reawakened African American musical traditions and heritage. Indeed, blues music helps Thomas remember how his mother used to sing to him. The music, however, is not merely for Thomas; it is needed by the whole reservation, which Alexie suggests is spiritually starved. Thereby, when the guitar plays itself, it satiates the environment itself: "The reservation arched its back, opened its mouth and drank deep because the music tasted so familiar" (24).

As the guitar leads Thomas, Junior, and Victor to form a band, Alexie makes apparent both the power of music as a transformative medium and how music itself can be a significant means through which to achieve real, significant power, beyond the reservation. As the reputation of the band grows, the increased attendance and fervent interest of the crowds make it a "semi-religious ceremony" (33), which threatens the various religious denominations on the reservation. It is no accident that Alexie describes the music of Coyote Springs as being semireligious since a significant portion of *Reservation Blues* concerns religion on the reservation, specifically the Catholic and Jesuit influences, subjects I will address later in this chapter. Still, the music they play may be antireligious, for it provides an outlet to express dissatisfaction, whereas most religions (especially Western religions) tend to dissipate dissatisfaction. It is significant that Christian Indians protest the band's rehearsals as playing the devil's music—which Victor proudly announces it is—because Alexie shows how music frees the reservation while religion, in a way, keeps it enslaved.

While at the beginning the music they play is primarily blues and rock influenced, in time it turns louder, quite aggressive, and more punklike, an assertive rebellion against the confining status quo. The band members refuse to play the role of the noble savage or wise, benevolent, exoticized other that non-Indians want them to be. This frustrates the expectations of non-Indians, whom Alexie describes as New Agers, as they hope to hear "ancient Indian wisdom" and instead hear loud renditions of the quintessential punk band, the Sex Pistols (40). Still, wherever there is prominent Indian culture, Alexie reasons, there are bound to be non-Indians who stereotype it as tame, spiritual, and nature-based while aiming to capitalize on it for their own personal well-being or wealth. Two such individuals are Betty and Veronica, white women who, it is revealed later in the novel, claim a dubious Indian heritage through a grandmother. Co-owners of a bookstore in Seattle, Betty and Veronica are drawn to all things Indian, but their efforts are for naught as their blond hair and excessive use of Indian jewelry distinctly set them apart from real Indians. In a way, Betty and Veronica are pale simulacra of the band, "songwriters" who write such vapid lyrics as "Indian boy, don't go away / Indian boy, what did you say?" (42). However, by sheer dint of being white, they become popular on the Spokane Indian Reservation, especially with Indian men who, Alexie suggests, are in large part drawn to white women because of their own internalized feelings of inferiority as Indians in a country that implicitly, and possibly explicitly, favors whites. Indeed, they become on- and off-again girlfriends of Junior and Victor, both of whom are drawn to white women.

One positive result of the music that the band plays is its ability to efface the boundaries between Indian tribes and reservations, which is not seemingly possible by any means other than music. The powerful music excites the Indian audience, which longs for power and hope, while it taps into subverted feelings of rage and powerlessness. Music is especially important in Indian communities, which Alexie describes as being primarily nonverbal. The importance and transformative possibilities of the band lie in the name that Thomas chooses for them: Coyote Springs. From Thomas's journals, we see the conscious ambiguity involved in his choice of the name Coyote Springs. The coyote is a canid related to the wolf, a trickster, and, according to Native American mythology, "responsible for the creation of the earth" and some subsequent impudent acts (48). Similarly, Alexie sees the music Coyote Springs plays as having the ability to create stronger, more stable identities and empowerment for Indian communities. Thomas also points out that a spring is "a source of underground water." Likewise, their music (at least at the beginning of the band's career) is a life-affirming expression of subverted disillusionment; from out of the blues they play comes life. Thomas also notes that spring also means "to make a leap or a series of leaps, e.g., from stage to waiting arms of Indian and non-Indian fans." Using this definition, the music they play works as a bridge between cultures, a method to efface boundaries between not only Indian communities but also other ethnic groups.

When the newly dubbed Coyote Springs play at a Flathead Reservation in Montana, they encounter two Flathead Indians who call themselves Chess and Checkers Warm Water. With the names "Chess" and "Checkers," Alexie playfully alludes to the two of the most important blues record labels. The Chess brothers, who in 1952 began a subsidiary record label known as Checkers records, started Chess records soon afterward. Unlike Betty and Veronica, with whom they are, in some ways, doubles, Chess and Checkers form a real alliance and substantial relationships with Coyote Springs. In particular, Thomas is drawn to Chess, singing his newly written "Indian Boy Love Song" for her and then bringing her on stage to sing a duet. Unlike when Betty and Veronica sing with Coyote Springs, when Chess does, there is an immediate connection, although Alexie describes it in a tongue-in-cheek manner with Chess feeling "like a Flathead Reservation Cher to the Spokane Indian version of Sonny" (58).

With the eventual inclusion of Checkers and Chess into Coyote Springs, Alexie helps further counteract the accepted Indian archetype of the omnipotent warrior/superman. That Victor still subscribes to this chimera becomes apparent when he opposes the inclusion of Checkers and Chess because he considers Coyote Springs to be a "warrior band" (77). The irony of Victor's claim is that his "talent" as musician is in large part due to the fact that he plays Robert Johnson's guitar, which pretty much plays itself. Apart from his bravado on stage, Victor has no more intrinsic musical talent than Chess or Checkers (possibly less), but by dint of being a man who believes in a patriarchal system, he does not want women to have equal footing with him.

As time progresses, Coyote Springs's music veers even more toward rock and punk than blues, evident by the fact that they begin a concert at the Tipi Pole Tavern on the Flathead Reservation with a Kiss song. This is in some ways a fall from grace, for while punk and rock music does offer the group (and the audience) more immediate satisfaction in assuaging their internalized rage, it also helps them lose track of their idealistic purposes in resurrecting and maintaining Indian culture while bettering the personal and social conditions of Indians themselves. In short, they become somewhat selfish and individualistic. Through amplified rock 'n' roll / punk music, Coyote Springs discovers a newfound sense of power and influence over the audience. For the members of Coyote Springs, who are accustomed to feeling powerless all their lives, the power in being acclaimed musicians becomes irresistible. To a large extent, the power and popularity Coyote Springs experience lead to their eventual undoing, for the power comes to mean more to them than the music, and they eventually value their individuality more than the collective fate of the group, reservation, and Indians as a whole.

The response to Coyote Springs's growing popularity is mixed at best on the Spokane Indian Reservation. To appreciate the blues means to acknowledge disaster, pain, and sadness, which is something that most Spokanes on the reservation aren't able or willing to do, in part because some, especially the men, are too concerned with constructing and maintaining a strong outer image. This, to a large extent, forms Alexie's strongest criticism of Indians on the reservation, especially men, who refuse to acknowledge, confront, accept, and ultimately transform the personal pain and suffering that blues music evokes. Thereby, Thomas (and, by default, Alexie) suggests that African American culture is healthier than Native American culture—or at least than Native American culture on the Spokane Reservation— because most in the African American community enthusiastically accept the blues, which requires the strength to accept personal pain and suffering. Theoretically, Native American blues music could champion indigenous culture and even befuddle or hoodwink mainstream American culture.

However, their music creates more controversy and disdain on the reservation than it transforms lives. In an open letter in the local Wellpinit paper, tribal chairman David WalksAlong complains about Coyote Springs, calling Victor and Junior drunks and condemning the band for including Flathead Indians. Meanwhile, his nephew Michael WhiteHawk, a bitter ex-convict bodybuilder, beats up Junior and Victor as well as Betty and Veronica, who flee in terror. At the same time, Christians on the reservation complain about Coyote Springs's music as being sacrilegious. When Thomas talks to some of the protesters of the band, he mentions to them that everyone on the reservation used to like them, but the protesters tell him that was before they left the reservation. To some extent, they resent their success or feel that Coyote Springs thinks that they are better than those on the reservation. Non-Natives aren't all that more accepting of the music, especially Betty and Veronica, who want light-hearted, sappy love songs. Chess condemns Betty and Veronica for wanting to flee the group after they encounter protest, resistance, and violence, claiming that they "want the good stuff of being Indian without all the bad stuff" (184). She further condemns them as selfishly being interested in Indian culture only so as to help them with their own personal problems, providing them with a more satisfying personal identity and offering them aesthetic beauty in areas deemed by Indians to be sacred.

Still, this is not to suggest that the entire white world and reservation vilifies Coyote Springs. Rather, Alexie portrays the reservation as being bitterly divided about the band, resulting in fights between the two sides. While the group achieves a modicum of success in small towns throughout the Pacific Northwest like Missoula, Montana, and Ellensburg, Washington, reaching a high-water mark with their victory in a Battle of the Bands contest in Seattle, it is a mere drop in the bucket. The group realizes that in order to forge any significant social change or to achieve wealth and fame, they need to become commercially successful. Therefore, they send letters to record labels throughout the country, who immediately dismiss "Indian" music as noncommercial.

It is at this point that the novel veers toward magic realism once again as it does with the appearance of Robert Johnson and his guitar. Two record executives, Phil Sheridan and George Wright, from the ironically titled Cavalry Records, come from New York City to sign Coyote Springs. Sheridan and Wright, real historical figures who fought Indians and slaughtered thousands of the Indians' horses in the 1800s, first appeared in the novel during one of Junior's dreams in which he led a band of Indian warriors who were ultimately routed by soldiers commanded by General Wright. Wright subsequently sentences Junior to death unless he signs something, presumably a treaty, although it's never stated. When Junior refuses to sign the treaty, they kill him and the dream ends.[11]

Alexie doesn't completely demonize Wright and Sheridan, although they are clearly not meant to be sympathetic characters, especially Wright, who is the less sympathetic of the two. In fact, Alexie writes that had Wright and Sheridan not appeared, "Coyote Springs might have sat there in Thomas' house for years, silent and still" (188). Still, Alexie suggests that the cold-blooded manipulation of certain non-Natives continues in a new kind of war in the business world and entertainment industry, both of which are dominated by whites. Sheridan and Wright's duplicity becomes apparent when they tell Coyote Springs that they want to sign them to their label, while sending a devious letter to their superior, Mr. Armstrong, in which they admit their more materialistic desires, claiming that to gain a wider audience they could make Coyote Springs dress up as stereotypical Indian savages complete with war paint and feathers. Wright and Sheridan are reincarnations of American cavalry leaders; like Johnson, they appear as ghostly, seemingly immortal figures, but they have malicious intentions that put them in league with the guitar.

It is important to remember that Johnson's guitar, according to legend, is an instrument of Satan bought by Johnson with his soul so that he could be the best guitar player in the world; the guitar or the entity that it serves does not have beneficial intentions, and the possessor of the guitar is vulnerable to its power. Indeed, as time progresses, Coyote Springs becomes greedier, losing sight of their original desire to transform conditions on the reservation or to help improve the lives of Indians. Although Thomas initially claims to be focused on making music, he admits to Chess that he wants strangers to love him but he claims not to know why. In all probability, Thomas has somewhat internalized the warrior archetype of male authenticity on the reservation as he insists that Coyote Springs must come back to the reservations as heroes. Otherwise, he claims, the

Spokanes will not accept them or will trounce upon them as failures. Thomas may be rationalizing his own desire for fame, but his comment proves to be fairly accurate.

The pressure to be hugely successful proves to be too much for Coyote Springs. When Coyote Springs attempts to record their first songs at the Cavalry Records recording studio in New York City, they buckle under the pressure. In all fairness, the head record producer, Mr. Armstrong, who was dubious about the project from the start, doesn't give them much of a chance. After they falter during their first attempted song, Mr. Armstrong summarily concludes that "they don't have it" (226), and with those words effectively ends the recording career of Coyote Springs. Alexie leaves the reader with unanswered questions: Did Coyote Springs overstep their boundaries by lusting too much for power and fame, thereby neglecting their ethnic roots? Was their failure an act of just retribution? Or was it more the result of callous racism on the part of Mr. Armstrong?

For Phil Sheridan, the answer is clear: it was Coyote Springs's fault as it has always been the fault of Indians since the time he was a general in the nineteenth century. Sheridan represents the historically hostile, dishonest, and violent approach mainstream America has taken toward Indians, whereas Wright is more sympathetic and has the potential to change. According to Checkers, Sheridan comes to her room and tells her that they blew it, "by acting like a bunch of goddamn wild Indians" (236). He tells her that he's tired of fighting Indians but they won't surrender. What follows is either an imagined or actual sexual assault upon Checkers. In other words, Checkers may dream her assault by Sheridan. When the rest of Coyote Springs goes to the hotel room where Checkers is, Wright is there but he claims that Checkers only had a nightmare. When she comes to,

Checkers tells the members of Coyote Springs that Wright saved her, and Wright explains his behavior as payback for the misdeeds of his past historical personage or for the general treatment of Indians by non-Natives. Indeed, it is through Wright's character that Alexie suggests that accepting responsibility and acknowledging the settling of the country as a brutal colonization/genocide can improve mainstream American attitudes toward Indians, which tend to be either indifference or simplistic, base romanticization. Alexie explains Wright's transformation when he, for the first time, really looks at the members of Coyote Springs and considers the historical oppression and massacres of Indians by whites, of which he was a part. At this point, when he looks at Coyote Springs, "He saw the faces of millions of Indians, beaten, scarred by smallpox and frostbite, split open by bayonets and bullets" (244). When he looks at his own hands, Wright sees bloodstains, symbolically representing his part in the massacres. Taking responsibility as a nation for prior historical massacres, even possibly a genocide, Alexie suggests, is the most important step toward reconciling American Indians and other Americans (especially members of the ethnic majority).

Ironically, it is when Coyote Springs returns to the reservation after they fail as a commercially viable musical group that they begin to get death threats. The residents of the reservation either resent that the group got their hopes up or they see Coyote Springs as weak and thereby easy prey that they can use to counteract their own internalized feelings of inferiority. Near the tribal community center, Christians picket with signs that call for Coyote Springs to be saved, while the nonreligious picket with aggressive, threatening putdowns of Coyote Springs. The extent to which the abrupt rise to "fame" and subsequent meteor-like fall affects Coyote Springs is most apparent in Junior, who becomes consumed by memories of a former girlfriend, a white co-ed whom he loved and who carried his child but who left him and had an abortion because her parents didn't want her involved with anyone of Native American descent. Junior, feeling he has nothing left, subsequently commits suicide. To some extent, the guitar is responsible for the ultimate undoing of Junior and the rest of Coyote Springs. It stalks Victor, promising him that with its help he can be or have anything, but he must "give up what you love the most" (255). Indeed, this is the same demand made of Johnson. Like Junior, Chess too feels extreme despondency after coming so close to achieving fame and success. While the guitar and the band inspired a newfound confidence, sense of self, and passion within her, it grew too fast, too soon, and, she later tells Thomas, "consumed almost everything" (257), including all the members of Coyote Springs. In other words, with help from the guitar, Coyote Springs got so caught up in the desire for fame and power that they became greedy and individualistic, which helped lead to the group's demise.

While Coyote Springs disintegrates in Spokane, the record executive, Phil Sheridan, hatches a new plan to capitalize on Coyote Springs without using them. For Alexie, Sheridan's act of appropriation is typical behavior of most non-Natives, who take whatever they like of Indian culture for their own profit or enjoyment. Sheridan proposes to Armstrong that, even without Coyote Springs, they can still capitalize on "Indian" music by using Betty and Veronica instead. That Wright rejects Sheridan's plan and repents shows how he has changed as a character/ghost. Wright ends up going back to his cemetery where he is "buried" and tells his dead wife that he killed Indians in what he now acknowledges to be massacres, if not part of a larger genocide.

However, Sheridan, who is in many ways the physical embodiment of the guitar and thereby an agent of Satan, preys on Betty and Veronica, telling them they can have anything they want if they disingenuously masquerade as Indian. He says they are in "the dream business" and that they "ask for a little sacrifice in return" (272). With this, Alexie somewhat demonizes the entertainment industry, which he suggests perverts the minds and identity of contemporary youth. When Betty and Veronica send Thomas a copy of the song they recorded for Cavalry Records, Thomas believes it will become a number-one hit, which indirectly implicates American pop music as preferring style/image/fluff over substance/content. The song itself is a hollow simulacrum of westernized Native American music (which is itself a simulacrum). The chorus of the song reveals that its intended audience is non-Native: "It don't [sic] matter who you are / You can be Indian in your bones" (295). For Alexie, the contention in the chorus of the song is an ultimately poisonous American ideal: that a person can be anything he or she wants to be, including another ethnicity, snatching whatever culture appeals to him or her without having to experience ethnic discrimination and racism. It also further oppresses a historically underserved ethnic group by taking from them the two main things that they have left to empower themselves: their identity and culture.

Another means with which mainstream America keeps the reservation and its residents placated if not enslaved is through religion. Throughout *Reservation Blues,* Alexie makes parallels between music and religion in the sense that both have ultimately been corrupted into personal pursuits for power and transcendence. Christianity plays a prominent role on the reservation as the religion impressed upon Indians by white missionaries.

Alexie contrasts Western religion with Big Mom, the unacknowledged matriarch and possibly religious leader of the reservation.
In part, Alexie's intent is to criticize and subvert Christianity,
which he perceives to be a tool of the ruling class (primarily
whites) to keep Indians, especially Indian women, enslaved. From
the priest who molests Victor when Victor was a child to the
Flathead Reservation priest, Father Arnold, who responds to
the romantic advances of Checkers, Alexie portrays (Caucasian)
priests as tormented by repressed sexuality and also drawn to
the priesthood because of the power it offers them, in a way
similar to which contemporary would-be musicians like Coyote
Springs are drawn to music because of its power and for the
possibility of celebrity.

One of the problems with Western religion on the reservation is that it fosters a sense of inadequacy in Indians, who
are taught to idolize religious figures portrayed as white in por-
traits and literature. Checkers admits that one of the reasons
she desired to be white when she was a child was that she had
always been exposed to pictures of Jesus as a white male. This
makes one of the songs Coyote Springs writes, "My God Has
Dark Skin," especially important. This song indicts Christianity
as not only subverting Indian traditions (cutting off traditional
Indian braids) but also silencing opposition and individuality.
Furthermore, Thomas describes himself as a "recovering Catholic," his disdain in part motivated by the draconian policies of
the Catholic Church on the reservation, such as burning reservation books and records they deem to be immoral.

Alexie makes the connection between music and religion
more apparent by mentioning that Father Arnold had been the
lead singer of a band when he was younger, before he had decided to join the priesthood. To a large degree, Father Arnold is

drawn to the priesthood because of the power it affords. When he moves to the reservation, he does little to improve conditions there. In fact, Alexie emphasizes that, above all else, he "loved his newfound power" (164). Indeed, for Thomas, Christianity is a method by which to control Indians, just as the rock music Coyote Springs plays toward the end of their short-lived career is basically an attempt to control, influence, or manipulate the audience. Later in the novel, Alexie describes both Father Arnold and Coyote Springs as performers who "wanted to be universally loved" (287). This compulsion ultimately leads to their downfalls. Father Arnold falls apart through his relationship with Checkers, which makes him question his integrity and makes him want to leave the reservation.[12]

Forming something of a polar opposite to Father Arnold and Christianity is Big Mom, whom Alexie describes as a matriarchal, authentic Indian alternative to the paternalistic, white hegemony of Christianity. A hodgepodge of tribes and a virtual legend unto her herself, Big Mom represents the tribe's spirituality, and the extent to which she has become isolated on the reservation (like Thomas), living by herself at the top of Wellpinit Mountain, shows how Western religion and culture have overtaken the tribe's cultural heritage. With Big Mom, Alexie also fights fire with fire, by reappropriating aspects of other cultures the way he perceives mainstream American culture has appropriated certain aspects of Indian culture and traditions. As established earlier, Alexie describes Big Mom as a musical genius who taught many of the most acclaimed contemporary American musicians. At the same time, Big Mom appears to possess superhuman powers as she is able to read thoughts, at one point accurately identifying that a priest had molested Victor when he was a child. Big Mom is not truly an omnipotent deity, however.

Rather, Thomas describes Big Mom as a bigger part of God, ultimately claiming that she is human but somewhat larger than life.

Ultimately, Alexie presents Big Mom as the unacknowledged leader or legislator on the reservation who is excluded because of the patriarchal hierarchy of the reservation. Big Mom champions artistic and cultural developments while most of the male-dominated reservation prizes the aggressive, warrior spirit. The true voice of wisdom in the novel, Big Mom wonders why Indian role models are almost uniformly male warriors, leaving no room for artists, leaders, and women. In a way, Big Mom fights especially for Indian women, like Chess, whose identity has become subverted in a male-dominated society (both on the reservation and in mainstream America). Later in the novel Chess comes to a realization that, throughout her life, men—from her dominating father and the priests to past boyfriends and the male leaders of Coyote Springs—have perpetually oppressed her. Yet Chess stays with Thomas in part because she has no real alternative if she wants to be with an Indian man. On the deteriorating reservation, large numbers of men have become unemployed alcoholics, which forces Indian women to lower their standards if they desire to marry an Indian man. Still, Alexie doesn't ultimately want Indians to completely reject Western ideals, culture, and religion. Instead, he seeks to find a middle ground between the two, evident toward the end of the novel, when both Father Arnold and Big Mom join forces at Junior's funeral.

At the same time, some of the characters do not see much opportunity or reason to establish connections between Native and non-Native cultures. Earlier in the novel, when Thomas, Checkers, and Chess find Junior and Victor naked in the van with Betty and Veronica, their relationship bothers Chess and Checkers, who call Junior and Victor traitors to their own DNA. This is not to suggest that Alexie rejects interracial romance, for Thomas's pragmatic and ambivalent response is that while love ought to be celebrated in any form, the children of interracial couples suffer tremendously at reservation schools, bullied and beaten up by "full-blooded" Indians. Indian men's desire for white women further oppresses Indian women, who live in a patriarchal society in which the patriarchs of that society often don't desire them. Rather, they long for white women as trophies or as a form of a revenge against white men.

Ultimately, Alexie suggests that the greatest threat to the reservation may be "Indians" of mixed ethnicity. When Chess sees a white woman with a child of mixed ethnicity, she is dismayed, predicting that the child will grow up to be conflicted, torn apart by his competing ethnic ties and isolated by both the Indian and white worlds. Furthermore, Chess foresees the "mixed bloods" as eventually taking control of the reservation "because they look white. Because they're safer" (283). In part to counteract this trend, Chess chooses the full-blooded Thomas as her romantic partner. Still, Alexie reserves hope for the renewal of community and strength though the literal and figurative character of Big Mom. Symbolically, toward the end of the novel, during a community feast, Alexie includes a playful satire of the miracle of Jesus's multiplication of the loaves and fishes. In Alexie's updated version, Big Mom, faced with potential chaos due to having only one hundred pieces of fry bread for two hundred people, comes up with the simple solution of tearing the bread in half. Alexie thus suggests that if the reservation strongly bonds together, placing community concerns over personal concerns, it can counteract poverty and despondency. That Robert

Johnson ends up staying on the reservation also suggests that there is room for cultural exchange between different ethnic groups.

While Johnson stays on the reservation, Chess, Thomas, and Checkers move from the reservation into the predominantly white city: Spokane. Their trip to the city is an uncertain one, but it does suggest that Alexie believes that some Indians ought to try to find success in the mainstream, white world rather than stay on the often stifling reservation. As they leave the reservation, Alexie describes the ghostly appearance of horses keeping pace with their van. Those horses can be seen as a symbolic representation of Indian culture, which the three need to keep with them in order to keep themselves culturally and spiritually intact in the city. In fact, Alexie describes the horses as both following and leading them into the city. With the final suggestion that "songs were waiting for them in the city" (306), Alexie implies that they will be able to resurrect their musical career in Spokane, but this time, without the crutch of Johnson's guitar, purely on the strength of their individuality and with help from their indigenous culture.

CHAPTER 5

Indian Killer

Whereas *Reservation Blues* was in large part gentle in its social criticism, often presenting Indians as resilient survivors and utilizing comedy to diffuse anger, pain, and tragedy, Alexie's next novel, *Indian Killer* (1996), is an uncompromising look at rage, anger, and violence both in the Indian community and in the larger world. In *Reservation Blues,* Alexie argues that ethnic hybridity can often be a space of productive creation, but in *Indian Killer* that same hybridity turns violent and destructive. In an interview, Alexie explains the initial genesis of the novel, dating back to when "I was sitting at Washington State [University] with frat guys in the back row who I wanted to kill. And I would fantasize about murder."[1] Alexie further explains how his own anger and dissatisfaction motivated the writing of *Indian Killer:* "It was a response to the literary movement where a lot of non-Indian writers are writing Indian books. Non-Indian authors enjoy a success that is not determined or critiqued by American Indians. So I want to make sure they're aware of an Indian critical response to their work."[2] Indeed, through his criticism of Clarence Mather, a white professor of Native American studies, and other pseudo-Indian fiction writers like Jack Wilson, Alexie does exactly that.

Whereas Alexie's previous works met almost universal praise, reviews of *Indian Killer* were mixed, presumably because of the sometimes graphically violent subject matter. In a review of the book, *Time* magazine called Alexie "septic with his own unappeasable anger."[3] With his characteristic humor, Alexie shrugged off *Time*'s criticism, telling an interviewer that, "I got a T-shirt with the quote on it. I loved the reaction. In some masochistic way, I love the really violent reviews more than the good reviews."[4] Still, Alexie claims that *Indian Killer* "was the hardest to write" of his works to date and that it "troubled" him the most, but it is also the book he "probably cares most about."[5]

More common were mixed reviews from critics such as John Skow, who describes the novel as "sad and eloquently written" but "also ugly," accusing Alexie of further polarizing ethnic groups.[6] However, such a viewpoint simplifies Alexie's novel, which may be pessimistic and vilify white society but also vilifies aspects of Indian culture and attitudes. While it is clear that Alexie's sympathies lie more with Indians, he does not excuse or endorse their actions and attitudes. Indeed, the ambiguity of the novel is apparent in the title, which can be read as an Indian who kills or an individual, presumably nonwhite, who kills Indians. In that, the title manifests a veritable circle of violence, which the novel itself plays out.

The protagonist of *Indian Killer* is John Smith,[7] an Indian who was adopted by a white couple, Daniel and Olivia Smith, themselves incapable of having children. For Alexie, a good deal of the novel's tragedy stems from the adoption. In an interview, he explains: "I've met a lot of people like him [John Smith] —'lost birds'—Indians adopted out by non-Indian families— we call them lost birds. . . . The social problems and dysfunctions of these Indians adopted are tremendous. Their suicide rates are off the chart, their drug and alcohol abuse rates are off the chart."[8] Indeed, the fictional protagonist, John Smith, was adopted at a time (in the 1960s) in which Indians were sometimes coerced into adoption since "until the passage of the Indian Child Welfare Act in 1978, many religious organizations actively recruited Native American parents to give up their children for adoption."[9]

Olivia and Daniel, John's white adoptive parents, represent the well-intentioned ignorance and obliviousness that Alexie perceives in the relationships of certain non-Natives with and toward Indians. Olivia and Daniel are far from malicious; rather, they are more like vapid pawns who subscribe to the ideas of the cultural majority without really thinking anything through. Olivia, a highly attractive white woman, is particularly narcissistic and oblivious, more a blank slate than an individual, who has never had any real ambition other than to be artistically cultured and wealthy. They decide to adopt a baby not because they are altruistic but because they cannot have one of their own and because they feel that at their age, it is socially proper to have a child. Daniel, the well-meaning but ultimately ineffectual father figure, tries his best to interest John in sports and in Indian culture, but Daniel lacks authority; he is unwilling to give up on John as a basketball player even though it turns out that John has no aptitude or even great interest in the sport. Furthermore, when John becomes a teenager and plays loud Native American music, which clearly disturbs Daniel, Daniel cannot confront John about it. In a way, Olivia and Daniel are products of a politically correct culture. Wanting to do the socially accepted right thing by exposing John to Native American culture, they both inundate John with all the information they learn about Indians and take him to Indian functions in order to expose him to "his culture." They even insist that an Indian Jesuit baptize John. However noble their intentions might be, Daniel and Olivia only serve to distance John from the Indian world, which in part excludes him because of his adopted white parents and because John, who does not know anything about his biological parents other than that his mother was fourteen when he was born, cannot claim heritage from any single Indian tribe.

All this leads John to misguided beliefs about Indians and whites. When Daniel and Olivia take John to an all-Indian basketball tournament, John misinterprets and romanticizes the various Indians of different tribes. He interprets their frequent laughter and joking to be evidence of their security and happiness when it is more like a self-defense mechanism to stave off despair. Along similar lines, as John gets older, he further romanticizes reservation and Indian life as well as his own feelings of ostracism. John's perception of Indians as noble savages may be informed by the overdramatic descriptions of Indians and their culture in the books that Daniel and Olivia give him, many of which were probably written by non-Natives without much or any direct knowledge of reservation life. *Indian Killer* begins with a chapter appropriately called "Mythology" in the sense that it is John's overly self-conscious elevation of his adoption into tragedy. John imagines being stolen by white people from his mother at birth, taken by a man in a jumpsuit into a helicopter, who randomly fires on people in the reservation, igniting a mini-war, while John is brought to his adopted white parents. No doubt the actual adoption process was significantly more innocuous than John would like to believe.

In other chapters of *Indian Killer,* Alexie identifies how John idealizes life on the reservation and imagines his biological family to be loving, strong and mutually supportive. In John's vision, everyone in the family eats well and as a unit; the children are taught Indian culture, and there is no conflict whatsoever between anyone. John's wizened grandfather tells stories while John dutifully prepares for college, planning to be a doctor and to later practice on the reservation. Missing from John's portrait, of course, is violence, alcoholism, rage, extreme poverty, and humor, all hallmarks of reservation life as Alexie details it in his previous works.

While it is undeniable that John is somewhat mentally unstable, at the very least, Alexie leaves it unresolved as to how much John's problems are genetically or socially based. That John often has trouble distinguishing between fantasy and reality indicates psychosis. In addition, his consuming paranoia toward virtually everyone and the imaginary voices he hears indicate possible schizophrenia. He even believes that there are several different Olivias and Daniels, all of whom are in some way out to get him. Further evidence of John's instability includes how, at twenty, John believed himself to be pregnant, a psychotic fantasy he takes to the point of buying birthing supplies. While Daniel and Olivia try to treat John's problems by getting him to take pills and threatening institutionalization, they are ultimately too weak as parents, in some ways probably fearing John. Despite evidence to the contrary, Daniel describes John's behavior as merely "little teenage rebellions."[10]

To be fair, John's mental problems may be exacerbated by his social milieu, such as being the only Indian teenager at a private school—which Alexie himself has experienced—leading John to feel ostracized from others. John's exclusion gradually develops into feelings of inferiority in contrast to the other white students, whom he deems to be more intelligent and complex than himself. To some extent, the attitudes of others cause John's feelings of inferiority. When John dates white girls, their parents view John with suspicion and subtly disapprove of their budding relationships. Like Daniel and Olivia, John's teachers are often overwhelmingly acquiescent of his frequently erratic behavior, never realizing that their response to John also makes him feel further isolated. When John gets into a fight, the principal lets John go without even a reprimand because of his ethnicity. To some extent, his teachers have good intentions in that they realize that, being an orphan and an Indian in a predominantly white school, John has a much more difficult time than most, but like Daniel and Olivia, John's teachers' seemingly good intentions actually evince a stereotypical and demeaning attitude toward Indians, whom they dehumanize in their generalized pity. What they don't realize or understand is that John, although adopted, comes from a wealthy family, and that one cause of his social problems are actions like those of his teachers that make him acutely aware of his ethnicity, which, because of his adopted status and his lack of knowledge about his biological parents, he has to deny.

In part motivated by how he is treated by people like his teachers, John attempts to find a sense of authenticity as an Indian. However, his attempts at authenticity are something of a masquerade, based on what John believes to be Indian role models, but whom John is drawn to because of their envied fearlessness: Mohawk Indian steelworkers who worked on the World Trade Center in New York City. Thereby, John becomes a construction worker, fully embracing anything deemed by the mainstream to be "Indian" because he has no real cultural identity, complicated by the fact that "tall and muscular, he looked like some cinematic warrior, and constantly intimidated people with his presence" (32). Ironically, John appears like a stereotypical image of an Indian, but culturally he is more Caucasian than Indian. Seeking power and acceptance from both the white and Native American worlds, John begins to lie to other people, telling whites that he is of Sioux origin "because that was what they wanted him to be," and telling Indians that he is Navajo "because that was what he wanted to be." John is not only aware of how intimidating he can be, he comes to believe that he could "rule the world" if he would dress as a stereotypical, savage, bellicose Indian (40). This is symptomatic of his delusions of grandeur. In fact, because he has lost his Indian heritage, John overdramatizes its power to the point of virtual omnipotence.

Complicating matters is that John appears in some ways traumatized by his Jesuit upbringing. Throughout the novel, he obsessively thinks of Father Duncan, a Spokane Indian Jesuit priest, who plays a significant role in John's childhood in adding to his vehemence against non-Natives by convincing him that white people killed most of the Indians but Indians did not kill all the white people because "they didn't have the heart for it" (14). Although Duncan vanishes after John turns seven, he remains an important mental fixture in John's life, whom John consults during his search for a stable community and for an otherworldly being like Bigfoot, whom he actively seeks and admires as a quintessential trickster figure.

John's reality is much different than his fantasy. The real-time narrative of *Indian Killer* in the present finds John, age twenty-seven, a reclusive, antisocial construction worker who avoids virtually all human contact. His ostracism is at least partially self-imposed, a product of his emotional instability, but also due to being Indian without having a definitive tribal identity in a predominantly white society. In part due to his internalization of the Indian archetype of men as warriors, John fantasizes about terrorizing the foreman of his construction company. Furthermore, his perception of Indians as having otherworldly power over nature (such as calling on the wind to strike at his perceived enemies) originates from Western stereotypes. In a deluded, possibly psychotic haze, John decides that he needs to kill a white man. Alexie thereby entices the reader to suspect that John himself is the Indian Killer, as he will with virtually every character in the novel. While John believes he is capable of killing a white man, he also realizes the futility of doing so, even on a large scale. John rationalizes his murderous desire as retribution for crimes against Indians, but in truth he is mostly driven by anger due to personal feelings of isolation and powerlessness. John's rantings have some sense to them, however, such as his claim that "white people no longer feared Indians" (30). Indeed, to mainstream white America, there is more of a perceived threat from the larger African American community, especially evidenced by riots of the past forty years, than there is from Indians. Alexie depicts John wanting to achieve power by frightening whites. To some extent, this may be part of Alexie's purpose in the novel. That is, he may feel that through fear, Indians can achieve some progress in social equality. John, however, desires whites to fear him more for his own personal benefit.

Another major character whom Alexie gradually implicates as a possible suspect for being the Indian Killer is Marie Polatkin, an undergraduate at the University of Washington and radical leader of the Native American Students Alliance. According to Ron McFarland, Alexie chooses the surname Polatkin because it "associates [her] with Chief Polatki, one of whose daughters was married to Qualchan, who led the Spokane, Palouse, and Coeur d'Alene tribes in 1858 against Colonel Wright."[11] Marie, a hot-tempered Spokane Indian activist, organizes protests against university policies that discriminate against Indians, such as a prohibition against powwows. As with John, Marie's anger and isolation are products of both Native American and white society. As a gifted, motivated student who knows very little about Spokane culture, Marie was immediately ostracized on the reservation, deemed to be not wholly Indian. It is important to recognize that John is not the only Indian struggling with how to achieve a sense of individual authenticity. Not only is Marie involved in the same struggle, so are all Indians, Alexie suggests, by obsessively ranking each other on the basis of how authentically Indian each is, determined not only by ethnicity but by knowledge of cultural traditions and purposeful isolation from the white world. Marie becomes convinced that in order to be happier, she needs to find other Indians whom she determines to be less authentically Indian than herself. Indeed, this is what ultimately drives her to be a Native American student leader at the University of Washington.

Alexie first entices the reader to believe that John is the killer when he has a streetside confrontation with a white man he accidentally bumps into. The condescending, possibly racist white man calls John "Chief," and when John doesn't say anything, the white man calls him a drunk and patronizingly asks if he needs help. The white man's blatantly assertive behavior infuriates John, reminding him of the many times he has felt powerless in his life. Alexie ends the chapter, however, by telling the reader that John follows the young man but not that he kills him. Rather than tell the reader this, Alexie maintains the mystery of the killer with third-person omniscient chapters written about or from the perspective of "the killer."

When Alexie describes the murder itself, he makes it sufficiently ambiguous by describing the prelude of the murder through a third-person omniscient narration of the "killer" who has a streetside confrontation with a white man similar to the one John just had. Still, streetside confrontations are sufficiently common that the killer could certainly be someone other than John. Whether or not the killer is John or someone else, Alexie makes him or her have the same difficulties distinguishing between fantasy and reality that John has and the same desire for power and to inspire fear. While Alexie writes that "the killer had not necessarily meant for any of it to happen" (53), the killer also takes pride in the kill by scalping the man. Furthermore, the killer derives a sadistic joy from murder as well, one that seemingly cannot be satiated, concluding that "one dead man was not enough" (54). The killer then leaves what becomes a trademark signature: two owl feathers.

The killer aspires to act like an owl, and Alexie chooses the owl feathers for their symbolic significance. As Bobby Lake-Thom explains, "The Owl is considered a bad sign and a bad power by most Native American tribal groups. It is a messenger of evil, of sickness, or of a fatal accident. It is also considered a sign of death."[12] Along similar lines, Alexie explains that the killer begins to consider the murders to each be part of a larger "hunt" and the scalping to be "trophies" or proof of a perceived power over whites. However twisted the killer's logic might be, he or she is not fully deranged and there is some method to this killer's madness. Later in the novel, the killer decides to kidnap a young white boy, Mark Jones, which proves to be a relatively shrewd terror tactic as it frightens families throughout Seattle. In a way, the kidnapping of Mark Jones mirrors John Smith's own imagined kidnapping at the beginning of the novel, which does lend evidence to the theory that John Smith is the killer.

Ultimately, the killer desires attention and overdramatizes his or her actions by claiming that the murders, the scalping, and the kidnapping of Mark Jones are the beginning of "the first dance of a powerful ceremony that would change the world" (192). Ultimately, the killer plays a cat-and-mouse game with the authorities. That the killer is not fully insane or murderous is evident in the surreptitious return of Mark Jones to his mother, past the not very watchful eyes of the police. However, returning Mark Jones does not denote a real change in the attitude of the killer, who, not long afterward, proceeds to mercilessly kill a businessman, Edward Letterman, ignoring Letterman's pleas for his life, even "feasting on his heart" before scalping him (328).

While the killer is the obvious villain of the novel, he or she is not the only one. With the character of Clarence Mather, a white professor of Native American studies, Alexie creates a metaphorical murderer, one who destroys, twists, or appropriates Indian culture and tradition for his own selfish devices. To some extent, Alexie uses Marie, a student in Mather's Native American literature class, as a mouthpiece against the teaching of Native American studies by non-Natives and also as a critique against the many fraudulent works of Native American literature actually ghostwritten or written by whites. Alexie describes Mather as a "Wannabe Indian" and, through Marie's critical eye, lampoons his reading list for the course as derived from misguided Euro-American conceptions of Native Americans and primarily designed for non-Natives as evidenced by the fact that Marie is the only Indian student enrolled in the class (58). When looking at the syllabus, Marie criticizes Mather's inclusion of *The Education of Little Tree* (which she believes to be written by a former Ku Klux Klan grand wizard) as well as *Black Elk Speaks, Lame Deer: Seeker of Visions,* and *Lakota Woman,* which she believes to be either ghost- or co-written by whites.[13]

In response to Marie's frequent, heated objections, Mather tries to defend his choices and course as "viewing the Native

American world from both the interior and exterior" (60). However, Marie continues to object to Mather's choices, claiming that "a non-Indian can't present an authentic and traditional view of the Indian world if he isn't authentic and traditional himself" (66). It is important not to mistake Marie's views for Alexie's views, although they may be similar. Alexie portrays Marie as somewhat of a victim of her own background, and thus she may not be a completely accurate mouthpiece for Alexie, especially considering that Alexie describes her motivations for objecting to Mather as being partially selfish, rooted in her own recurring personal struggles and her own need for conflict, which has become a nearly constant element in her life.

While Marie thrives on conflict, she also is at least partially altruistic, as evidenced by her volunteer work for homeless Indians in Seattle, many of whom call her "The Sandwich Lady" because of the food she provides for them. Still, Marie's rage is also directed toward Indians, many of whom she accuses of frittering their money, time, and energy away during powwows or other "celebrations," which she believes to be fraudulent and especially indulgent considering the many destitute and hungry Indians who could be helped with the time and money that other Indians devote to powwows. Alexie wants the reader to believe that, given Marie's rage, she also could be the Indian Killer, a possibility suggested by Marie's explosive reaction to a person, Boo, who helps her deliver food to the homeless. When he suggests that they use mayonnaise on the sandwiches, Marie has a near violent reaction due to a concern for money, and Boo tells her that she sounds like the Indian Killer. In addition, when Boo asks Marie, half in jest, whether she is the Indian Killer, she ducks the question, never answering it. Furthermore, Marie's growing obsessive disdain of Mather, which leads to stalking him on more than one occasion, appears borderline pathological or psychotic.

For Mather, the situation with Marie reaches a breaking point after weeks of confrontation. Mather's ignorance becomes increasingly apparent with such claims as "gambling casinos on Indian reservations are very much an act of fiscal rebellion," which Marie convincingly refutes by calling them "a financial necessity" (83). While Mather insists that, through his course and his research, he attempts to provide an uplifting account of Indians, he is obviously blinded by his own conception of Indians (even if it is positive) and, at one point, sternly slams his office door in Marie's face during one of their after-class confrontations. Alexie further entices the reader to consider Marie as the Indian Killer with a description of how infuriated she feels after Mather shuts the door in her face—to the point of wanting all whites to "disappear," wanting "to burn them all down to ash and feast on their smoke" (85). Even if Marie is not the Indian Killer, Alexie's intention is to show how Indians commonly experience violent rage and anger due to marginalization, discrimination, and unequal power struggles. This, for Alexie, is much more of an accurate generalization than depicting Indians as benevolent and nature-loving or warrior/savages.

Another character who is more of a probable suspect as the Indian Killer, given his violent tendencies, is Marie's cousin, Reggie Polatkin, at one time a close friend of Mather's. With Reggie, Alexie shows how being of mixed ethnicity can be as trying, if not more so, as having no biological parents (John Smith) or being full-blooded but ostracized (Marie). Again vilifying whites, Alexie describes Reggie's white father, Bird Lawrence, as violently racist toward Indians, whom he believes to be ignorant savages. He forces Reggie to use his Indian mother's surname and refuses to let him use the surname Lawrence until Reggie displays sufficient docility toward him. Bird's abusive behavior, demonstrated by calling Reggie a "stupid, dirty Indian" when Reggie does poorly in school (94), leads Reggie to harbor feelings of anger and inferiority. Consequently, over time Reggie comes to prize his white ancestry, considering it to be responsible for his successes, while he vilifies his Indian ancestry, holding it responsible for his failures.

Only after Reggie takes a class with Mather does he become interested in Indian culture, but his interest, piqued by Mather, is misguided and becomes merely a facade. Together, the two attend traditional Indian cultural events like sweathouses, where Reggie discovers that being Indian offers him power over the other whites who attend and look to him for instruction and guidance. Consequently, he begins to act wise, all-knowing, and domineering. Alexie suggests that Reggie's experiences are not unique and that many Indians subscribe to mainstream codes for identity, which supplant their real identity, for doing so offers them rewards from non-Natives.

Still, it is Mather, rather than Reggie, whom Alexie ultimately vilifies as immoral and unethical. Their breaking point occurs when Mather finds audiotapes of Pacific Northwest Indian elders recorded in 1926. He plays them for Reggie, who insists that the tapes be erased because they are family stories, not meant for public consumption. While Mather wants to publish articles about the tapes, Reggie not only wants to keep the tapes from the prying hands of whites like Mather, but, like Mather, he also wants to keep the tapes for himself. To some extent Reggie's rationale is understandable, but it is extreme. Rather than considering giving them to a neutral third party, Reggie lets his anger and rage get the better of him. Mather is no better. In fact, his behavior is worse. After Reggie confronts him about the tapes, Mather denies their existence because of greed and selfishness. In Mather's deluded world, he comes "to see those stories as his possessions, as his stories, as if it had been his voice on those tapes" (138). Mather's extreme immorality can be seen in that he continues to lie to the department chair about the existence of the tapes after Reggie lodges a complaint, leading Mather to selfishly keep the tapes for his own personal listening pleasures.

Furthermore, Alexie lampoons academic posturing and rationalization through Mather, who actually absolves the "Indian Killer" of responsibility and thereby denies him or her any agency. By blaming "capitalism," Mather's pseudo-Marxist rationale ignores race and ethnicity while theoretically encouraging the killing, as is demonstrated by his calling the Indian Killer a "revolutionary construct" (245). Losing the ability to take anything literally, Mather sees metaphors and representation when there really aren't any and makes sketchy analyses of the killings. Mather also represents poor literary analysis of the novel itself, evidenced by when he describes the kidnapping of Mark Jones as a metaphor for the Indian condition, an attempt to counteract centuries of oppression. Alexie, who in his poetry has previously lampooned literary critics for seeing metaphors and symbols in his work at places in which there aren't any or for overextending their meaning, uses the same technique here.

With Mather, Alexie also considers to what extent a non-Native can really be an expert of Native American studies. That Mather has, as he points out to Marie, lived on a reservation for several months and assisted the AIM movement during the late sixties and early seventies, improves his credibility. However, as a wealthy, white American, he lacks the firsthand knowledge of racism, discrimination, poverty and feelings of powerlessness. In essence, he is in too privileged a position to truly understand the "Indian condition" as he generalizes it.

While Mather is obtuse, arrogant, and immoral, he is not or does not appear to be physically violent, unlike most of the Rogers family, composed of the father, Buck, and two sons, Aaron, a vicious, violent ringleader, and David, a student in Mather's Native American literature class, who is thought to be killed by the Indian Killer but is actually killed by two random white men. The Rogerses own land near an Indian reservation and David recalls how Indians would "trespass" on his family's farm when David was a child to take camas root, "a traditional and sacred food of the local Indians for thousands of years" (62). David's father, Buck, having no use for camas root or the land where it grows, refuses to allow the Indians access to the land and the roots. Unconcerned about these Indians (and presumably all Indians), the Rogerses ironically regard them as trespassers, even shooting at them when they "invade" their land. Buck defends their actions to his children by claiming he is protecting his land from thieves. Buck, of course, doesn't realize the irony in his claim since the land was originally stolen from the ancestors of these Indians.

Representing far-right conservatism at best and a vicious, cold-blooded racist at worst, Truck Shultz, a white talk-show host reminiscent of Rush Limbaugh, helps stir up anti-Indian sentiment during the time of the killings. That Shultz, who espouses pro-white and anti-Indian rhetoric and is also the most popular talk-show host in the city, evinces a stern critique of Seattle, where the novel is set. Comparing Indians to spoiled children and savages, Truck claims that "we have coddled Indians too long and we've created a monster" (209). Truck, in many ways, is the most one-dimensional of all the characters in *Indian Killer*, which may be understandable given that as a radio talk-show host, his stage identity may have usurped his real identity.

What is shocking then, is the extent of Truck's popularity. Even the seemingly innocuous Daniel Smith listens to Truck. Alexie implicates the city of Seattle for its lack of diversity and lack of equal opportunity for minorities. He describes Seattle as merely having a veneer of diversity when the city itself is largely ethnically segregated, with minorities residing in one part of the city and whites living in another. Further complicating matters is the friction between different minority groups. John Smith, for instance, recognizes common ground between himself and African Americans but finds it impossible to connect with the two African American men (Paul and Paul Too) who work at Seattle's Best Donuts, where he is a frequent customer.

That Seattle is an ethnically polarized city becomes even more apparent as ethnic violence erupts after the police and media start calling the killer the "Indian Killer." Certain whites, angry at perceived attacks against them by the "Indian Killer," proceed to taunt and attack random Indians. Aaron Rogers, with two of his friends, leads random violent attacks against Indians as retribution for the murder of his brother David (although, as Alexie later reveals, he was not killed by Indians). Still, Alexie doesn't portray in a much better light extremist Indians, who, in their thirst for blood, glorify the Indian Killer as being a contemporary reincarnation of Crazy Horse, Chief Joseph, Geronimo, and Wovoka. One cheers on the killer, as in a sporting event in which the score is "ten million to three, in favor of the white guys" (220). Furthermore, Reggie assaults whites as mercilessly as Aaron Rogers does Indians.

Meanwhile, John grows steadily more unstable and, in his delusion and haze, becomes convinced that one death will rectify the wrongs committed against Indians. While this would seem to lend credence to the theory that John is the Indian Killer, the fact that he insists on a single death and the Indian Killer has already killed more than one person make the possibility that he is the Indian Killer less likely. Another suspect is Jack Wilson, an "Indian" mystery writer whom Mather assigns in his course and who also functions as a double of John Smith. Wilson's romanticized, misguided depictions of Indians can be seen through his protagonist, Aristotle Little Hawk, a Shilshomish Indian, shaman, and private detective in Seattle. Little Hawk possesses the stereotypical features of Indians, "a hawkish nose, walnut skin, and dark eyes," as well as a savage, emotional instability (162). It is significant that when Jack Wilson encounters John, he thinks John looks exactly like his fictional hero, Little Hawk, because Jack and John are virtually alter egos, their generic first names variations of the same name and both possessing generic last names. Furthermore, like Aristotle, John Smith is all image and little or no substance, looking like a stereotypical Indian but internally possessing no real authenticity. Like John, Wilson is an orphan, isolated as an adult, and while Wilson is white and John Indian, they both overly romanticize Indian life and culture because they both believe that it offers a nurturing, supportive environment where all are welcomed (in contrast to how they view mainstream American society). Similar to John, Wilson conceives of himself as a romantic loner who is "in search of his family" (157).

Furthermore, just as John pretends to be from a certain tribe, Wilson concocts a half-baked story about having an Indian relative so that he can claim he is of mixed ethnicity. Alexie's sympathies lie more with John as John cannot fit into either the white or Indian world, whereas Wilson could easily live as a white man if he chose to do so. Alexie also uncovers the hypocrisy that allows whites to claim Indian status with a mere modicum of Indian ancestry (a reverse form of the one-drop rule), whereas Indians with a modicum of white ancestry, such as Marie, cannot really pass as white. When Wilson goes to an Indian bar (Big Heart's), Alexie points out Wilson's ignorance in that Wilson does not recognize that class distinctions do not matter as much as tribal distinctions to Indians. While Wilson believes himself to be accepted by other Indians at Big Heart's, he also does not realize that they are merely patronizing him and surreptitiously mocking him.

Still, in contrast to Alexie's depiction of racist police officers, Wilson appears almost heroic. Here, Alexie once again implicates Seattle; this time for discrimination and racism within the police department. When homeless Indians are killed, one officer tells a disconcerted Wilson that the crime isn't really worth being investigated and the perpetrator ought not to be actively sought because he views killing Indians as "pest control" (160). However, now that the victims are white and the perpetrator presumably Indian, the police take immediate action. Had the killer been a minority, Alexie suggests, there would not have been nearly as much concern, especially if the victims weren't white. Supporting this idea is the fact that there is an outpouring of grief for David after he is found dead, whereas there is little or no concern for the Indian victims of Aaron's and other whites' rampages. In addition, whereas the police trust the testimony of a white man who was beat up by Reggie and his friends, when an Indian man reports an assault at the hands of whites, the officers believe he is probably delusional.

That most people insist that the Indian Killer is Indian is somewhat justifiable given the scalping and owl feathers, but it is by no means a certainty. While the police insist that an Indian is the killer, Wilson mentions that many non-Indians know about scalping. Furthermore, it is the common perception that an Indian is the killer, preying on white people, that sparks the extreme fear in Seattle, a fear Alexie would argue that Indians experienced during the settlement of the country and that, to some extent, they continue to experience up to the present day. While Wilson realizes there is a possibility that the "Indian Killer" is not Indian, he doesn't believe that possibility. However, it is conceivable that Wilson may be the killer himself, evidenced by how, in one dream, he thinks of John as the killer and then "Wilson saw himself with that knife. Wilson saw himself pushing the knife into one white body, then another, and another, until there were multitudes" (391). At the same time that Alexie suggests Wilson may be a possible suspect, he makes it less likely that John is the Indian Killer. At one point in the novel, two white men threaten John and Marie and then attack John. While John at first threateningly waves a golf club at the white men, he inexplicably gets frightened, screams, and runs away. In contrast, Alexie portrays Marie as more capable of violence. After learning of the random violence committed against Native Americans in Seattle, Marie is so infuriated that she "wanted to tear out their blue eyes and blind them" (375).

Aaron Rogers and his friends mainly commit these random acts of violence as supposed retribution for the death of Aaron's brother David, whom they mistakenly believe to have been killed by the Indian Killer. However, Aaron is not the only one responsible for inspiring the violence. Truck Shultz could also be held responsible due to his anti-Indian rhetoric and for boldly announcing that the Indian Killer was responsible for Edward Letterman's death before possessing any legitimate evidence, leading to violence and rioting in Seattle.

Meanwhile, John decides that Wilson is the person who needs to be killed. Since Wilson is a virtual double of John, John's desire to kill Wilson may be a veiled desire to commit suicide, which he eventually does instead of killing Wilson. That Wilson keeps insisting to John that he is "Indian," not white, demonstrates how he has come to believe his own lies. Therefore, when John wonders "if Wilson knew the difference between dreaming and reality. How one could easily become the other" (403), it is clear that Wilson does not, especially as a writer. John comes to the conclusion that "Wilson was responsible for all that had gone wrong" (404). In essence, Wilson represents the desire on the part of certain whites to usurp Indian identity, and it is that same desire which may have led Daniel and Olivia to adopt John in the first place. It is not so much that Wilson is responsible for "all that had gone wrong," as John claims, but rather, like Mather, he is a metaphorical vulture plucking the last remnants of Indian identity and culture. John then slashes Wilson's face on the twisted, irrational logic that it will prevent him from claiming Indian ancestry because John believes the scar will forever mark him as an imposter and a symbol of white theft and perversion of Native culture.

After John's death, the police prematurely think of him as the chief suspect for being the Indian Killer, although they have no hard evidence linking him to the crimes. Wilson capitalizes on the incidents by writing a book about John, concluding, like the police, that John was the Indian Killer. Thus, even Wilson's disfigurement is not enough to counteract his distortions of Native American culture. That Wilson ends up being the ultimate authority on the killings is ironic, for it is in his literary nature to only obfuscate any illuminations of Indian life. Indeed, Wilson becomes even more arrogant after John's death as Wilson comes to believe not only that he is the only one who can understand who and what motivated the Indian Killer (whom he believes to be John) but that his book would "finally reveal to the world what it truly meant to be Indian" (338). Similarly, Clarence Mather also capitalizes on the killings, writing a book about it and claiming that Reggie and possibly Marie were behind the killings. That Aaron Rogers and Barry Church only get six months in county jail for their violent assault and near-killing of several Indians in Seattle shows even more racial discrimination in the Seattle judicial system.

Some critics take fault with Alexie's uncompromising ending, which they interpret as justifying or glorifying violence against whites. At the end of the novel, an Indian, possibly the killer him- or herself, performs a Ghost Dance. The Ghost Dance, over five hundred years old, was performed in hopes that it would dispel the invading whites and resurrect dead relatives and loved ones, while returning the land to a precolonized state.[14] Earlier in the novel, Marie had castigated Mather for not understanding the full rationale behind the Ghost Dance. Whereas Mather views it as a benevolent, symbolic act, Marie interprets it literally as an expression of anger against the historical oppression of whites to the point of wanting them banished forever from the continent. Mather claims that the Ghost Dance was "about peace and beauty" (313), but Marie claims it is more about retribution and that in the late twentieth century, given the decrepit state of reservations and of Indian life both on and away from the reservation, there is more reason than ever to feel angry at the oppression of whites and to support the Ghost

Dance. In the last chapter, during a final vision, when the killer begins to perform the Ghost Dance, other Indians (hundreds) come and dance it along with him. Alexie describes the killer as planning on "dancing forever" and that the surrounding trees grow "heavy with owls" (420). As established earlier, according to traditional Indian folklore, the owl is a sign of evil, sickness, or death. Alexie thus suggests that the killings will continue in the future. This is not to suggest that Alexie encourages an attempted violent revolution, for he surely recognizes that such an attempt would ultimately prove futile, but that the desire for revolt and revenge remains an important, albeit repressed desire for many Indians, a startling revelation for many who believe in the stereotype of Indians as docile, despondent, and nature-loving.

CHAPTER 6

The Summer of Black Widows
and One Stick Song

Despite its rather ominous title, *The Summer of Black Widows* (1996), a collection of poems and prose poems, is a return to the more personal and immediate. Rather than considering the intersection points between Native and mainstream America as in *Reservation Blues* and *Indian Killer*, Alexie returns primarily to an exploration of reservation life. The poems often celebrate the strength and resilience of cultural traditions in the face of poverty and marginalization while offering ideas for empowerment of the Indian community.

As in his previous collections of poetry, Alexie emphasizes the importance of imagination and storytelling as having the greatest potential for ameliorating conditions on the reservation. It is he, the storyteller, who asks an unnamed person if he can "weave a story / from your hair" in "After the First Lightning," which helps them to remain "warm and safe" from the metaphorical storms that batter the reservation.[1] In the title poem, "The Summer of Black Widows," Alexie compares stories to black widow spiders, thereby emphasizing their potential for violence and destruction. It is these dangerous, threatening spiders that descend upon the reservation; however, "the elders knew the spiders / carried stories in their stomachs" (12). The spiders/stories that appear dangerous are actually benign: "The stories rose on hind legs and offered their red bellies to the most beautiful Indians." Alexie suggests that people on the reservation fear stories just as they fear black widow spiders, but their fear is ultimately groundless and counterproductive. He notes that "We captured stories / and offered them to the ants, who carried the / stories back to their queen / A dozen stories per acre / We poisoned the stories and gathered their remains with broom and pan." Ultimately, they poison the stories because they fear the vulnerability that would come by hoping once more and by trying to retain their cultural traditions. However much some might try to ignore or debase the power of stories, Alexie suggests that the stories are ultimately indestructible, needing only brave individuals to locate them: "The elders knew the spiders / had left behind bundles of stories. / Up in the corners of our old houses / we still find those small, white bundles / and nothing, neither fire / nor water, neither rock nor wind / can bring them down" (13).

The challenge to the reader in many of Alexie's poems is how to discern—or whether it is indeed possible to discern—if the speaker is Alexie himself and whether the poems ought to be considered as autobiography or fiction. That Alexie's poetic mission statement is Poetry = Anger × Imagination suggests that there is a distinct element of fiction in his poetry. Alexie, an extremely self-reflexive writer, is himself aware of the reader's difficulty in distinguishing fact and fiction in his writing. In the tradition of the trickster, he may want to purposely frustrate the reader and prevent him or her from categorizing his poetry as invention or autobiography. In the poem "Father and Further," seemingly an account of his relationship with his father, Alexie plays the role of the trickster when he writes: "Of course, by now, you realize this is a poem about my father. It could also be a series of exaggerations and outright lies. I might be talking about another man who wears my father's mask. Behind that mask, he could be anyone" (41). That Alexie never resolves this one way or another forces the reader to remain in a state of disequilibrium. He doesn't want the reader only to interpret the poem as autobiography, for to do so would prevent the reader from generalizing and discerning larger meanings from the poem.

Alexie toys with the elegiac form in "Elegies," which he describes as "a poem for people who died in stupid ways" from Custer to Japanese blowfish eaters to smokers. Whereas the poem at first appears macabre and condescending, Alexie shifts gears and includes himself, or at least the person he used to be, in the poem. He writes, "This is a poem for me. No. This is a poem for the me I used to be, the me who once drove drunk on purpose, knowing I was too drunk to drive well, quite sure I might die in a crash. I was the me who changed his mind halfway through the ride, stopped the car in the middle of the road, and walked home" (50). In that sense, the poem can be read as a wake-up call to others living in ignorance, a means of preventing these senseless "stupid" deaths. That most of these deaths or near-deaths were preventable seems to place the blame on individuals themselves. Ultimately though, Alexie casts blame or places the responsibility upon the Indian community. The poem concludes: "This is a poem for my tribe, who continue to live in the shadow of the abandoned uranium mine on our reservation, where the night sky glows in a way that would have invoked songs and stories a few generations earlier, but now simply allows us to see better as we drive down the highway toward a different kind of moon" (51). In other words, Alexie recognizes that the Spokanes need to break the cycle of monotony and impoverishment but that this won't be possible through just a summer of black widow stories; rather, it can only be accomplished through long-lasting mental changes and by learning

how to prioritize cultural traditions over personal aggrandizement. That being said, Alexie realizes the difficulties in doing so,
given the poverty of the reservation, which forces economic concerns to be placed above cultural ones.

Still, nobody ultimately is safe from Alexie's scorn, certainly
not reviewers or critics, one of whom he lampoons in the poem
"Fire as Verb and Noun." In this poem, Alexie, the trickster,
actually de-emphasizes metaphorical meanings of the poem and
frustrates critics who overstretch the meanings of his poems. The
poem begins with an epigraph, a overwrought literary analysis
from *Publishers Weekly* that claims: "Working from a carefully
developed understanding of his place in an oppressed culture,
he [Alexie] focuses on the need to tear down obstacles before
nature tears them down. Fire is therefore a central metaphor: a
sister and brother-in-law killed, a burnt hand, cars aflame" (52).
This epigraph is immediately followed by another one, presumably from one of Alexie's friends (Donna Brook) who read the
review and responds: "Sherman, I'm so sorry your sister was
killed by a metaphor." Alexie, whose poetic praxis lies close to
that of the confessional school, does not necessarily choose
words or images for their metaphoric possibilities; rather, many
of his poems are emotional purgings of real-life events. His common use of fire is not primarily symbolic but rather inspired
by the real-life events of his sister's and brother-in-law's deaths.
To write about fire is thus to manage grief, to mourn, to remember, and to come to terms with this painful event. Alexie
suggests that there may be some cause-and-effect relationship
between fire and what it consumes. His somewhat macabre
thought is whether or not the color of the flames "that rose / off
my sister's and brother-in-law's bodies" were "the same color"
(53). Furthermore, he wonders, "Could I change the color of the

flames / if I emptied the contents of my shopping bags / onto the blaze?" Alexie is driven to obsession with fire because it has wounded him through the death of his sister. He asks the reader or critic from *Publishers Weekly,* whom he accuses of pseudo-intellectualism, of robbing the poem of its emotional power: "What do you do / when your sister burns / like a bad firework?" (55). He finishes the poem with another seeming response to the critic: "There is a grave on the Spokane Indian Reservation / where my sister is buried. I can take you there." Once again, this poem demonstrates Alexie's dictum that Poetry = Anger × Imagination. In this case, Alexie lets his imagination run wild, wondering what exactly happened during the deaths of his sister and brother-in-law, in either an attempt to manage his grief or an example of his obsessional thinking.

In either case, Alexie questions his own persistent and recurring desire to learn as much as he can about their deaths. He wonders if he has taken his imagination too far, if in fact he has come to focus obsessively on the deaths. He writes: "Have I become an accomplished liar / a man who believes in his inventions? / When I see my sister in every fire, / is it me who sets her in those pyres / and burns her repeatedly?" (60). In essence, Alexie wonders if he tarnishes the memory of his sister through his self-described obsession. This can be read in two ways. Either Alexie lies about seeing his sister in every fire to dramatize the importance of it to the reader, or his imagination deceives him by obsessively showing him his sister in every fire.

Similarly, in the poem "The Exaggeration of Despair," Alexie either criticizes himself for sensationalizing Indian misfortunes as devastation or the title is a self-reflexive, sarcastic commentary written in the voice of a non-Native who does not realize or comprehend the bleak economic and emotional realities. Perhaps Alexie "exaggerates" by focusing on the most desperate Indians: a girl whose brother has just committed suicide and whose older brother attempts suicide as well, an Indian man raped by priests, an Indian woman who was sold "for a six-pack and a carton of cigarettes" (96). Alexie ends the poem with "I open the door / and invite the wind inside" (97), as if he is shutting himself off to these exaggerated images.

Still, at worst Alexie is no more guilty of exaggeration than most poets, which isn't nearly as bad or destructive as the mainstream American public or media, who not only marginalize and oppress Indians but also help foster stereotypes of Indians. In "How to Write the Great American Indian Novel," Alexie takes aim at publishers and marketers who help perpetuate stereotypes of Indians in literature. The poem is a mockery of the desired components of an Indian novel, requiring Indians to have "tragic figures" and showing racism in their requirement that "the hero must be a half-breed" (94). In their stereotypical account of Indians as noble savages, the authors of these books always compare both men and women to nature, with the dictate: "Indian men are horses, smelling wild and gamey" (95). Not only do all Indians have "visions," according to this praxis, white people can "carry an Indian deep inside themselves," revealing that the true audience for "the great American Indian novel" is definitively white. It becomes clear at the end of the poem that Alexie's great American Indian novel as portrayed in the poem is a sham, reflecting the appropriation of Indian culture and identity by whites, which leads toward their gradual subsumption and even destruction. Ultimately, fiction may replace fact, for it is this fictional ethos that may become a reality. Alexie concludes at the end of the poem: "In the Great American

Indian novel, when it is finally written, / all of the white people will be Indians and all of the Indians will be ghosts" (95).

Alexie's unclear, at times hostile relationship with his audience is further complicated by the poem "Tattoo Tears," which begins "No one will believe this story I'm telling, so it must be true" (56). By this logic, the reader would only believe the unbelievable. However, Alexie may once again be playing the role of the trickster. The poem insists that the average reader will not be able to comprehend or sense any hidden depths. Therefore, an Indian woman tattoos three tears "under her left eye folded under the weight of her own expectations, after her real tears failed to convince." For Alexie, the tattooed tears are necessary because he believes Indians have been denied their basic humanity and that their pain is not recognized but rather ignored. Furthermore, American mainstream culture implicitly forces minorities to be subservient and/or invisible. The real tragedy, as Alexie identifies it, is that Indians are often complicit, allowing their identity to be subsumed. He writes:

> Disappear, father, as you close your eyes to sleep in the drive-in theater. What did you tell me? *Movies are worthless. They're just sequels to my life.* Disappear, brother, into the changing river, salmon traveling beneath the uranium mine, all of it measured now by half-lives and miles-between-dams. Disappear, sister, like a paper cut, like a rock thrown through a window, like a Fourth of July firework. (57)

In response to this neglect, Alexie writes poetry to bring attention to what is often forgotten. However, even Alexie questions whether poetry ultimately can make a difference because it can't make real something or someone that only the writer knows or has experienced. "If I show you the photograph of my sister just emerged from the sweat house," he wonders,

> steam rising from her body like horses, a single tear tattooed under the right eye, can you pretend to miss her? . . . If I show you the photograph of my sister in her coffin, hair cut short by the undertaker who never knew she called her hair *Wild Ponies,* will you imagine you loved her? (58)

However, Alexie's intention is not merely to forge an emotional response in the reader. Rather, it is to overcome a desperate situation. He writes in a single line in part 12 of the poem: "Imagination is the only weapon on the reservation." The reservation has been clouded by popular culture that passes as "reality," for "in the reservation Kmart, forty televisions erupt in a 20th century vision: 500 years of bad situation comedies" (59).

In response to the deterioration of Indian culture, some of Alexie's poems celebrate or try to reawaken that lost heritage. At the same time, he displays a strong environmentalism. For instance, in "That Place Where Ghosts of Salmon Jump," Alexie tells a creation story concerning one of the most ancient mythic symbols for most Native tribes, the coyote, which is "often portrayed as either the creator or the trickster."[2] In the poem, Alexie imagines Coyote created Spokane Falls, "that place where salmon swam larger than any white man dreamed" (19). However, Alexie's Coyote, as is sometimes the case with traditional Native symbols of the coyote, is a trickster figure, not necessarily benevolent. In fact, Coyote creates the Spokane Falls out of anger for feeling isolated. In this poem, Alexie's sympathies lie not with the mythic symbol, Coyote, but with the true creators, the storytellers. The speaker proclaims, "Coyote, you're a liar and I don't trust you. I never have / but I do trust all the stories the grandmothers told me." He calls on Coyote to witness the deterioration of nature and despoliation of the environment at the hands of non-Native settlers and interlopers. He tells Coyote to "look at the Falls now and tell me what you see. Look / at the Falls now, if you can see beyond all of the concrete / the white man has built here." The speaker dismisses mainstream American culture, which, as Vine Deloria Jr. has argued, tends not to believe in the intrinsic sacred qualities of the environment, whereas traditional Indians, having a different conception of the environment and having lived on the land considerably longer, have direct religious and personal ties to the environment.[3] "Coyote," the speaker calls out, "these white men sometimes forget to love their own mothers / so how could they love this river which gave birth / to a thousand lifetimes of salmon? How could they love / these Falls, which have fallen farther, which sit dry / and quiet as a graveyard now?" Furthermore, the speaker bemoans the sterility and abject conditions of the sacred land: "These Falls are that place / where ghosts of salmon jump, where ghosts of women mourn / their children who will never find their way back home, / where I stand now and search for any kind of love, / where I sing softly, under my breath, alone and angry." He calls on Coyote for help to transform the land back to its former state.

Along similar lines, Alexie explains how the Spokane Indian Reservation was ransacked and plundered at great environmental cost due to the discovery of uranium on the reservation and the subsequent mining and stripping of the area by non-Natives eager for quick, easy money. The poem "Halibun" describes how the uranium on the Spokane Indian Reservation was discovered, and Alexie suggests that the carelessness of the operation and the aftereffects of uranium mining led to the release of carcinogens and the eventual deaths of many on the reservation. He notes, "I cannot tell you how many coffins we filled during the time of the trucks, but we learned to say 'cancer' like we said 'oxygen' and 'love'" (29). Unconcerned with the environment since it is not their home, non-Natives leave an environmental mess after they finish mining, complete with "pools of dirty water, barrels of dirty tools, and mounds of dirty landfill. They taught us 'dirty' meant 'safe'" (30). Alexie suggests that the mining of uranium on the reservation goes beyond physical degradation of the land and the legacy of environmental hazards, also deteriorating the culture of the residents, whose identity is directly connected to the land itself. He writes of the time after mining: "For decades, we Spokanes stared in the night sky with envy and built flimsy wings for ourselves." The situation won't be improved by the attempted quick fixes of those who despoiled the land. "Now in 1994," Alexie writes, "the white men have come back to clean what they left behind. They plan to dig deeper holes and fill them with fresh water. They plan to dump indigenous waste into those lakes, and then add waste shipped in from all over the country. They gave us a 562-page bible that explains we cannot stop them."

Still, despite the damage and impoverishment, Alexie depicts the reservation as a safe, nurturing haven in contrast to mainstream American society. In the poem "Tourists," he imagines James Dean, Janis Joplin, and Marilyn Monroe as visitors on the reservation, finding the peace and contentment that they couldn't find in the white world. James Dean comes to the reservation "in search of the Indian woman of his dreams" (91). Alexie claims celebrities, usually outsider figures, for the reservation, who he thinks embody the qualities of the reservation. Although "James Dean has never seen a powwow, . . . he joins right in, dancing like a crazy man, like a profane clown." Janis Joplin appears in the Powwow Tavern, at home with the other drunk Indians. In the most touching of the pieces, Alexie imagines how Marilyn Monroe would have found peace, even spiritual restoration on the reservation, a respite from the pressures and demands of mainstream America. In the poem, a drug-dependent Monroe comes to the reservation, and Native women take her through a purification ceremony. Whereas in mainstream America, the public would have ogled Monroe, and no doubt someone would have leaked her location to the media, this does not occur on the reservation. Rather, "Marilyn's prayers may or may not be answered here / but they are kept sacred by Indian women" (92). Alexie describes how he imagines the process of purification would have taken place: "At first, Marilyn is self-conscious, aware / of her body and face, the tremendous heat, her thirst, / and the brown bodies circled around her. / But the Indian women do not stare" (93). Alexie thereby suggests that there isn't the same obsessive focus on the body in the reservation as there is in mainstream America. Finally, Alexie describes the feelings of normalcy that Marilyn would only be able to feel on the reservation: "Marilyn is not Indian, Marilyn will never be Indian / but the Indian women sing about her courage. / The Indian women sing for her health. / The Indian women sing for Marilyn. / Finally, she is no more naked than anyone else." According to this poem, only in this nonjudgmental environment would Monroe feel restored.

Still, in other poems, Alexie looks to romantic relationships as possibly effacing ethnic boundaries. At the same time, in other poems, he shows how there are certain universals like food and sex that are stronger than ethnic identity. Unlike Alexie's previous collections, in *The Summer of Black Widows* there are more poems about a speaker's—presumably Alexie's—personal relationships. In "How We Learn to Say 'Mouth' and 'Hand' and 'Small of Back,'" the speaker addresses his Indian lover by asking, "Body to body / do we create / language?" (64). While neither speaks the tribal language, Alexie suggests that wordless, physical relationships are in some ways more substantial than any spoken language. Along similar lines, in the poem "Marriage," Alexie begins with the essential bond, which is sustenance, rather than ethnic identity. This poem begins with the claim that food is ultimately the single most important item for forming community: "What it comes to is this: bread. Its creation the product of hunger and imagination" (65). In this poem, Alexie makes distinctions on the basis of economic class rather than ethnicity: "Tribes have gone to war because of wheat and corn." For a change, Alexie seeks the universal, common experience shared by all people that effaces boundaries.

Still, ethnicity obviously means a good deal to Alexie, who confesses that he may have chosen his wife (who is in fact Indian) in no small part due to her ethnicity. In "Drum as Love, Fear and Prayer," he addresses a skeptical audience, whom he presumes would denigrate such a choice. To this hypothetical audience, Alexie asks: "If I choose to love / this Indian woman / mostly because she's Indian / then who are you to stop / this love between / an Indian woman and man?" (70). Since ethnic identity is central to Alexie, he chooses a partner who can share that crucial aspect of his being.

Not all poems in the collection are personal and romantic. As he did in *Indian Killer*, Alexie also displays a fierce, uncompromising side in "Capital Punishment," written from the perspective of a cook who has just made an Indian murderer his last meal before execution. The speaker (and possibly Alexie's sympathies) seem in part to lie, at least metaphorically, with the killer, whom he describes as having "pushed / his fist all the way down / a white man's throat, just to win a bet / about the size of his heart" (86). Obviously feeling vehemence toward whites himself, the speaker describes his small retaliatory actions: "For the boss I just cook. / He can eat what I put in front of him / but for the Indian man to be executed / I cook just right" (87). As Alexie does in *Indian Killer,* the speaker of this poem criticizes the prejudicial justice system, which convicts "mostly the dark ones / who are forced to sit in the chair / especially when white people die" (86). For the speaker, executions have become a possibly racist form of entertainment for the presumably white audience to prey on the typical minority figure, with "pollsters and secretaries / who keep track of the small details: / time of death, pulse rate, press release."

Still, Alexie is nothing if not a writer with myriad perspectives and voices. His account of reservation life in *The Summer of Black Widows* is somewhat manic-depressive, ranging from wild exuberance in his basketball poems and paeans to Walt Whitman to fierce, vengeful social criticisms of mainstream America. "Defending Walt Whitman" is an exuberant account of basketball on the reservation. Alexie praises basketball as providing a healthy outlet for rage and anger. In describing the basketball players, Alexie insists, "These are the twentieth-century warriors who will never kill" (14). In basketball, Alexie sees Whitman's spirit and energy, including him in a hypothetical game with Indians who are able to find the self-confidence and joy otherwise lacking on the reservation. Similarly, in "Why We Play Basketball," Alexie describes how important sports have become to the reservation, to the point that they will play in the depths of winter, melting snow from the court in order to do so. "We were Indians who wanted to play / basketball. Nothing / could stop us from that, / not the hunger in / our thin bellies, not / the fear of missed shots, / not the threat of white / snow" (21). Basketball is the only stable activity in their lives. Unlike their families, unlike other people, unlike their jobs (if they have one), and unlike the reservation itself, basketball remains an empowering constant. "In basketball, we / find enough reasons / to believe in God, / or something smaller / than God. We believe / in Seymour, who holds / the ball in his hands / like you hold your God" (23). Through basketball, a solid community is forged, providing the players with personal strength.

The poem "Inside Dachau" offers an important look into Alexie's literary evolution. In the poem, Alexie describes a visit to Dachau, and while there he wonders about the purpose of the restoration of concentration camps and why people (including himself) go to visit them. He asks himself, "Are we searching for an apology / from all of the Germans who refused to see / the ash falling in front of their locked doors? / Why are we here? What have we come to see / that cannot be seen in other countries?" (119). Yet Alexie realizes that monuments to genocides and massacres need to be maintained because public acknowledgment of their existence in museums and memorials can help prevent subsequent ones from occurring. Seeing Dachau makes Alexie conclude that America needs to acknowledge and construct monuments to the massacres and genocide of Indians. In response to the question of what do indigenous people want, Alexie writes, "We are waiting for the construction of our museum" (120). It is doubtful that Alexie will ever have this wish granted, since to construct such a museum would mean that Americans would have to acknowledge that the country was founded and settled through violence, murder, and greed. It is doubtful that the government, let alone most Americans, would be able to accept this because to do so would tarnish their patriotism and nationalism. From the last lines of the poem, in which Alexie writes, "I wonder which people will light fires next / and which people will soon be turned to smoke" (122), it appears that Alexie doesn't believe such a museum or acknowledgment is possible, either.

In "The Powwow at the End of the World," Alexie refuses to forgive and forget Indian massacres. In the poem, Alexie lists qualification after qualification for forgiveness, from the replenishment of the salmon in the Spokane River to a "fire / which will lead all Indians home" (98). Finally, Alexie concludes that he won't forgive until "I am dancing / with my tribe during the powwow at the end of the world." In other words, he will not forgive until either the end of civilization as we know it or until his reservation or the entire country returns to a precolonized state. The latter, of course, is next to impossible, and the former isn't exactly desirable. However, it reflects how strongly Alexie feels about remembering the past abuses, killings, and massacres of Indians, which he ultimately regards (at least in the poem) as unforgivable.

Alexie's uncompromising, confrontational tone continues in the concluding poem, "Bob's Coney Island," but it is softened by considering the amusement park at Coney Island and the joy that it provides children. The poem begins with a stern but obviously impossible demand: "Let's begin with this: America / I want it all back / now, acre by acre, tonight. I want / some Indian to finally learn / to dance the Ghost Dance right / so that all of the salmon and buffalo return / and the white men are sent back home / to wake up in their favorite European cities" (138). However, the speaker "hesitates" when he considers how important

Coney Island is to his tour guide, Bob, who was at one time "a 13-year-old boy / who believed that Coney Island belonged to him / though we know that all we see / doesn't really belong to anyone" (139). With this last thought, Alexie softens his demands, concluding: "I'll let Bob have a conditional lease / because I know finally / somebody will take care of this place / even if just in memory." Alexie thus concludes this collection somewhat ambivalent about the presence and influence of non-Natives in America.

One Stick Song

Alexie's most recent collection of poetry and prose poetry is *One Stick Song* (2000). As with his previous collections of poetry, it is difficult if not impossible to determine the extent to which the poems are autobiographical, a difficulty Alexie wants to foster so as to prevent his poetry from being read as merely confessional. Yet *One Stick Song* is Alexie's most personal work yet, from the frequent mentions of his actual wife, Diane, to poems concerning his father. To generalize, in this collection Alexie has moved from the external to the interior. Yet one thing remains constant: many of the poems evince a social outrage, even anger and hostility, which accords with Alexie's self-described praxis, repeated again in this collection as "Poetry = Anger × Imagination" (20). However, some reviewers fault Alexie for what they perceive to be overwhelming, ultimately obfuscating hostility. For instance, Donna Seamen, writing for *Booklist,* describes Alexie as expressing "an anger as large and molten as the earth's core; but like the earth, which conceals its heat beneath forests and oceans, he cloaks his with mordant humor and a rough-and-ready lyricism."[4] In her analysis, Seaman exaggerates, for the majority of the poems in the collection are self-reflexive, mournful, even whimsical, expressing little or no rage.

The first poem in the collection has a characteristically comic, almost paradoxical title: "The Unauthorized Autobiography of Me." Of course, a person writing an autobiography doesn't need authorization, for an autobiography by definition is self-authorized. Alexie may use this title because he doesn't want the reader to consider the piece to be true autobiography; that is, portions of it may be fictionalized, and certainly portions of it are not autobiographical at all. In fact, the "poem," composed of nonchronological, fragmented memories, descriptions, and ideas, begins with a description of a fierce basketball game on the Spokane Indian Reservation. "They will play until the brown, leather ball is invisible in the dark. They will play until an errant pass jams a finger, knocks a pair of glasses off the face, smashes a nose and draws blood."[5] From this description, Alexie concludes: "This may be all you need to know about Native American literature" (13). He thereby suggests that perhaps the fierceness, commitment, and drive with which they play basketball represents the larger, centuries-long struggle against colonialism that still exists today and, Alexie would presumably hope, will continue in the future.

One way Alexie believes that Indians will regain some power is in transforming the meaning of the ethnic label with which they have been historically demeaned: *Indians*. In "The Unauthorized Autobiography of Me," he writes: "Thesis: I have never met a Native American. Thesis repeated: I have met thousands of Indians" (13). When asked during a panel on Indian literature why Alexie prefers to call himself and others Indians, he explains that they want to "own" a word that once was used to demean them. "So much has been taken from us," he writes, "that we hold onto the smallest things left with all the strength we have."

In a way, the speaker of many of the poems (presumably Alexie himself) wants to reclaim his ethnic heritage as a result or in spite of his rather untraditional upbringing, evident in his family's mainstream predilections. His mother sings Donna Fargo songs, not traditional Spokane Indian songs, and the music they all listen to is mainstream white American music, which the speaker renounces to some extent. One long fragment of the poem describes attending a Kiss concert in Spokane, and the next fragment seems to be written in response, as if the present-day Alexie regrets his past and has subsequently recovered his ethnicity and heritage: "I made a very conscious decision to marry an Indian woman, who made a very conscious decision to marry me. Our hope: to give birth and raise Indian children who love themselves. That is the most revolutionary act" (17).

Alexie's greater belief in ethnic solidarity and the strict demarcation of ethnic lines become even stronger when he presents an "incomplete list of people" he wishes were Indian. This list, composed of athletes like Kareem Abdul-Jabbar and Mohammed Ali, film stars like Robert De Niro and Meryl Streep, as well as musicians, writers, and religious figures, shows that Alexie wants to keep the boundaries between ethnicities intact, although he desires to take what he perceives to be the best of other cultures. Yet, the fact that Alexie writes that he wishes they would be Indian doesn't mean that he insists they must be. Still, his respect for these individuals or regard, it is implied, would be greater if they were Indian.

One reason for Alexie's strict demarcation of ethnic boundaries is that he perceives mainstream America to be institutionally racist and prejudiced. One example of this is his criticism of the publishing and literary world for how it has shaped "Native American literature." Alexie claims that "a book written by a non-Indian will sell more copies than a book written by either a mixed-blood or an Indian writer," and that "Reservation Indian writers are rarely published in any form" (21). The irony of this claim is that Alexie himself has outsold many non-Indian writers, but granted, he is an exception to this rule. Furthermore, Alexie claims that non-Indian writers help invent a mythology and spiritual significance that may not actually exist but rather is a self-perpetuating myth. These non-Indian writers gloss over the abysmal conditions of Indians on the reservation, wanting to claim Indian ancestry for the personal benefits it would purportedly provide them while they still live a comfortable, mainstream existence far away from the poverty of the reservation. Alexie uncovers the hypocrisy of such people when he writes: "So many people claim to be Indian, speaking of an Indian grandmother, a warrior grandfather. Suppose the United States government announced that all Indians had to return to their reservation. How many of these people would not shove that Indian ancestor back into the closet?" (24). Ever the trickster, Alexie also mocks readers who confuse his fiction for reality. He recalls reading a story "about an Indian father who leaves his family for good. He moves to a city a thousand miles away. Then he dies. It is a sad story. When I finish, a woman in the front row breaks into tears" (25). When the woman says she's sorry about his father, Alexie responds: "Thank you, but that's my father sitting right next to you."

Still, most of the poems in the collection are starkly personal, some even despondent. This is illustrated best in the title poem, "One Stick Song." In an interview, Alexie explains the genesis of the poem as originating from a gambling game:

Someone was talking about this song he'd sing—"one stick song." You see, you lose sticks in this gambling game, like

> chips or whatever. You're down to one stick. And you're
> going to lose if you lose it, so this is your most powerful song.
> You're desperate. But I hadn't heard the phrase "one stick
> song" in years, and as soon as I heard it I thought, oh my
> God, that's everything I've been doing. "One stick song" is a
> desperate celebration, a desperate attempt to save yourself:
> putting everything you have into one song.[6]

Ultimately, Alexie notes that "It ended up being an elegy for all
the family members I've lost."[7] Toward that end, Alexie describes
each deceased family member in a verse of the poem, from his
sister, killed in a fire, to his grandfather, killed during the Second
World War. The purpose of this, and other poems like it, is not
merely for Alexie to purge personal grief but to remember and
praise these people who have greatly affected him. Rather than
purging grief, these poems focus on remembrance. In "The
American Artificial Limb Company," he calls his deceased sister
his "phantom limb" and describes his grief for her death as
unshakable and ultimately subsuming him (73).

   Along similar lines, the poem "Sugar Town" is a paean to
the speaker's—possibly Alexie's—father, who has been ravaged
by diabetes, his foot amputated. In a sense, the poem is Alexie's
reconciliation with his father, who was an alcoholic and with
whom Alexie had a rough relationship. As a new parent himself,
Alexie may perceive his father in a new light and see his own
personality mirrored in his father, such as in their shared "in-
ability to remain serious / between and among injuries" (88).
For Alexie, humor is one way to deal with grief, for as he claims,
"I must insist that everything is funny." Possibly to counteract
all Alexie's previous stories about his father or failed fathers, he
addresses the reader: "I love my father / with and without, on /

and off, the reservation. I want / you to know that" (89). Alexie would not want the reader to know this were he not concerned that the reader might have gathered a different impression from reading his work, an understandable impression considering the many poems he has written that contain alcoholic, rage-ridden, abusive father figures. Instead of placing himself in an external cultural tradition, Alexie places himself in a familial tradition; in other words, family has come to supplant ethnicity in importance. While the two are certainly related, the poems in *One Stick Song* do not make as much reference to ethnicity. One reason for this may be Alexie's experiences as a new father, which has no doubt changed his priorities. The poem ends with: "That cry in the night / is my son, is my father. / Both want me to be / a better man than I am" (91).

Mostly devoid of metaphors and similes, the poems are often simple, direct, and to the point. Sometimes Alexie's personal experiences inform his larger opinions. While many of his poems praise basketball, "The Warriors" denounces baseball, in fact beginning with Alexie's bold claim, "I hate baseball" (46). Although Alexie claims to hate baseball because of its faux-patriotism and for its faulty "reputation for magic and poetry," he admits his hatred stems from his own mediocrity in the sport. Unlike basketball, which he believes to inspire community and passion, Alexie describes baseball as exacerbating violence with fights frequently breaking out amongst the players. It is also in this poem that Alexie addresses his romantic and sexual development, indicating that as a teenager he grew to deify white women and dismiss Indian women. He blames television for this:

Television taught me that the bodies of white women were more beautiful than the bodies of brown women. Television

taught me that brown skin was inherently evil and dirty.
On television, white men were heroes and Indian men were
savages. I learned to hate my brown skin and came to believe
if I could touch the bare skin of a white woman I could somehow change myself. (48)

Also in the poem, Alexie discusses his relationships with white
women, describing his lust as a "dangerous bomb that constantly threatened to destroy any number of lives. . . . But, as I
grew a little older, I realized that I wanted to defuse that bomb.
I was no longer in love with my lust for white women" (49).

In *One Stick Song,* more than any other of Alexie's books—
with the possible exception of *The Toughest Indian in the World*
and *Ten Little Indians*—sexuality plays a significant role both in
the poems themselves and in the lives of those portrayed in
them. In "Open Books," Alexie argues that a significant aspect
of the poetic world and a significant draw for poets (especially
male poets) is the lure of sexual power. The poem begins, "Along
with the sonnets and blank verse / comes this: the gossip / about
which poet is sleeping / with which poet, about who left whom
/ for who" (29). Alexie's portrayal of academic poets is hardly
flattering, with one throwing a drink in the face of a female
undergraduate who refuses his sexual advances, while another
forgets or never bothers to learn the name of the woman he slept
with the night before, who comes to one of his book signings.
Sexuality is also another connection that Alexie recognizes to
be in many ways stronger than any ethnic identity. In "Sex in
Motel Rooms," Alexie writes about the anonymity of sexuality
and its ability to nullify identity. Meanwhile, in "Powwow Love
Songs" Alexie describes powwows more as mating ceremonies

than cultural ceremonies by detailing random sexual encounters there. Accordingly, the narrator chooses his clothing according to how he believes it will attract women there: "I will wear braids / if I want to attract an Indian woman who speaks / her tribal language. I will wear / a ponytail if I want to attract an Indian woman / who plays basketball. I will wear my hair loose and uncombed if I want / to attract an Indian woman / who will climb into a camper with me and teach me / about her dark body" (78).

However, Alexie also realizes that sexual desire can be extremely misleading, and those who have an especially weak identity or self-regard, as many in the Indian communities do, are especially vulnerable to sexual desire for people who appear to have a higher degree of self-regard or self-love (typically whites). This is the focus of the poem "Why Indian Men Fall in Love with White Women," in which the speaker claims to fall in love with a white donut-shop clerk because of her careless-ness, happiness, and obviousness, "because she laughs so joy-ously, because her eyes / are blue and alive with happiness and intelligence" (75). From this, the speaker decides that "she is indeed too clever to be / working in a donut shop," when in truth he has only been duped by her facade of contentment. When the white woman takes and eats a donut that the speaker offers, "she takes it with delight / and she bites into it / and chews it without suggestion. She chews simply / with and with-out grace" (76). That this woman has presumably never experi-enced hunger, racism, or abuse makes her appealing to the speaker, who presumably has experienced all these things. While Alexie admits to still lusting after some white women, "I know now that a white woman could never love me in the way an

Indian woman can. . . . I know now there is something redemptive in loving an Indian woman. I feel as if I'm somehow forgiven for my years of ignoring Indian women" (49). In a primary sense, *One Stick Song* is Alexie's personal celebration of coming to full intellectual and emotional maturity. At the same time, it is a collection about familial and ethnic reconciliations; in essence, Alexie gets back to his roots.

CHAPTER 7

The Toughest Indian in the World

With his next collection of short stories, *The Toughest Indian in the World* (2001), Alexie continues the exploration of sexuality that he began in *One Stick Song,* this time often examining homosexuality. Another major difference is that in this collection, Alexie primarily investigates Indians living in urban areas, a departure from his typical focus on the reservation. In his own words, Alexie explains what motivated his literary change of direction: "I've been reading recent Indian literature, and little of it is about urban Indians, despite the fact that most of us Indian writers are urban Indians now. I also wanted to get away from the model of the dysfunctional Indian."[1] To some extent, this is a natural development representing Alexie's own success as a writer and filmmaker and his subsequent exposure to the larger world. As he explains, "I've been living in the city— Seattle—for five years. I live a very cosmopolitan life now. I've traveled the world and had dinner with movie stars. To pretend that I'm just a Rez boy is impossible. Certainly, I think this book has much more of an urban perspective."[2]

The Toughest Indian in the World became Alexie's most critically acclaimed work since *Reservation Blues.* Sybil Steinberg, writing for *Publishers Review,* describes the collection as "revealing him [Alexie] once again as a master of his craft."[3] Donna Seaman, in *Booklist,* describes it as a "superb" collection: "His humor is swift and wry, his characters vital and complex, and his wild story lines express his clear-eyed view of Indian culture, his fury over racism and his deep and abiding belief in love."[4] Recognizing the humor and multiple layers involved in Alexie's writing, Joanna Scott, for the *New York Times,* describes *The Toughest Indian in the World* as "slam fiction," which lies "somewhere between a David Letterman monologue and a Flannery O'Connor story."[5] She also describes Alexie's stories as "designed to shock and usually revolve around an action a character perceives as transgressive."[6] However, Alexie's intention is not merely to shock the reader with "racist idiocy and historical injustice," as Scott claims.[7] One of his goals is also to deconstruct and possibly dismantle what he perceives to be Indian standards for (male) identity, typically revolving around aggression and hypermasculinity. The title of the collection reveals what many Indians, especially men, aspire to be, but in doing so they deny their vulnerability, their ability to think critically and to consciously decide on a more legitimate, individual identity. Furthermore, most who are unable to fit this mold are set up for failure and feelings of low self-worth and tend to feel isolated or excluded.

This is especially apparent in the title story of the collection, which involves a homosexual relationship between an Indian journalist and an Indian fighter. The journalist picks up a hitch-hiking boxer who has just fought a Flathead reputed to be "the toughest Indian in the world."[8] This Flathead fighter refuses to give up no matter how hard he is hit or injured, because, Alexie suggests, of his resilience and possibly also due to his lack of intelligence. The fighter eventually gives up and lets the Flathead win by sitting out the count. Hearing this story, the journalist is presumably impressed, considering the fighter to be possibly the toughest Indian in the world.

At the same time, the title of the story/collection may also apply to the narrator as well. The narrator's tough, almost impenetrable exterior shell mirrors that of his father, who uses his pessimistic resignation as a steely front against being emotionally hurt. The narrator recalls, "My father never taught me about hope. Instead, he continually told me that our salmon— our hope—would never come back, and though such lessons may seem cruel, I know enough to cover my heart in any crowd of white people" (21). It is easier to be "tough" like the narrator's father because to be hopeful means being vulnerable and risking pain, but acting "tough" is ultimately poisonous, evidenced by what he tells his son about white people: "They'll kill you if they get the chance. Love you or hate you, white people will shoot you in the heart." While there may be some truth or wisdom in what his father tells him about white people, to accept this would mean that the journalist would never really establish any significant relationships with whites (which turns out to be the case) and the gulf between the ethnicities would widen. To some extent, it is difficult to determine whether Alexie criticizes these characters for developing such a tough skin or attitude, for he has previously described being Indian as a struggle for survival. But their denial of vulnerability and hope results in mass disillusionment and also leads them to deny their imagination, which Alexie has previously described as the most important weapon against impoverishment and marginalization. As the journalist puts it, "For most Indians, stars are nothing more than white tombstones scattered across a dark graveyard" (22). In this categorization, most Indians have lost their romanticism in part as a defense mechanism but also due to their tough environment and to interethnic codes.

The irony of living amid white American culture and yet wanting to ignore it has not registered with characters like the journalist. The journalist claims that "Indians just like to believe that white people will vanish, perhaps explode into smoke, if they are ignored enough times" (22), and yet he is aware that most Indians celebrate certain white musicians such as Hank Williams, Patsy Cline (whom he calls their Virgin Mary), Freddy Fender, George Jones, and Conway Twitty, among others. Still, the journalist desperately wants to reconnect with Indians, especially considering that he is essentially distrustful of whites. Following in his father's footsteps, the journalist picks up only Indian hitchhikers, for no other reason other than they are Indian and hitchhiking. In essence, the narrator has become so acutely aware of ethnicity to the point that outward appearance has become virtually everything to him.

Outward appearance is also crucial to his conception of Indian masculinity, which to him is quintessentially aggressive, coarse, and thick-skinned, denying sensitivity and vulnerability. The journalist doesn't quite believe he matches up to this archetype given his white-collar profession and his sensitivity, evident in his account of a sexual relationship with a white woman, Cindy. When making love to her, the journalist would sometimes ask her, "How does that feel?" and considers himself to be "quite possibly the only Indian man who has ever asked that question" (24).

The hitchhiker/boxer the narrator picks up in his car appears to be the epitome of the stereotypical male Indian warrior that the narrator probably longs to be:

Long, straggly black hair. Brown eyes and skin. Missing a couple of teeth. A bad complexion that used to be much worse. Crooked nose that had been broken more than once.

Big, misshapen ears. A few whiskers masquerading as a mustache. Even before he climbed into my car I could tell he was rough. He had some serious muscles that threatened to rip through his blue jeans and denim jacket. (26)

Feeling disconnected from his tribe and heritage, the narrator, who moved away from the reservation twelve years prior and rarely goes back, is drawn to the fighter, possibly because he exemplifies his archetype of an Indian male. After the fighter tells his stories, the narrator tells him, "You would've been a warrior in the old days, enit? You would've been a killer. . . . I was excited. I wanted the fighter to know how much I thought of him" (30). Later, the narrator tries to impress the fighter by showing him his own tough skin and his own lack of romanticism: "I wanted to tell him that the night sky was a graveyard. I wanted to know if he was the toughest Indian in the world" (31). The irony of the story becomes apparent when the fighter, with whom the narrator shares a hotel room, precipitates a homosexual encounter by climbing into bed with the journalist, who does not resist the fighter's advances. Here, Alexie shows how the toughness is merely a facade, a sham, and to some extent may be symptomatic of repressed homosexual urges. For to elevate the male warrior figure on a pedestal means to sexualize him to some extent.

After the fighter leaves, the journalist believes himself to be tougher, to have somehow captured the essence of the fighter: "I threw a few shadow punches. Feeling stronger, I stepped into the shower and searched my body for changes. . . . I wondered if I was a warrior in this life and if I had been a warrior in a previous life" (33). However, the experience does not seem to change him; rather, he retains his rather poisonous grief: "At that moment, if you had broken open my heart you could have looked inside and seen the thin white skeletons of one thousand salmon" (34). Salmon, for the narrator and for Alexie himself, who both hail from the Spokane Indian Reservation, is a sacred fish that was once their primary means of sustenance. With this ending, Alexie suggests that the narrator is far from having grown stronger; he has actually grown emotionally vapid.

"The Toughest Indian in the World" is not the only story in the collection to deal with homosexuality. In an interview conducted around the time of the collection's publication, Alexie condemned homophobia as being "the only universally accepted hatred across all religions and cultures and it makes no sense."[9] At the same time, he praises—and at the same time generalizes —male homosexuals for their benevolence, asking the interviewer to "find me a country where gay men started war on straight men."[10] In part, Alexie implicates the Indian community for homophobia in their strict codes for male and female authenticity. He also deconstructs mainstream white narratives of dominance such as the romanticization of the typically male rebel/outlaw figure. In "South by Southwest," a parody of the outlaw narrative, Seymour tries to rob "love" by holding up an IHOP restaurant. The misguided Seymour seeks celebrity: "He wanted the local newspaper to give him a name. Seymour wanted to be the Gentleman Bandit" (57). Seymour's misguided romanticism, Alexie argues, is a privilege afforded to the non-oppressed. Hence, he writes that Seymour "was a white man and, therefore, he was allowed to be romantic." Instead of robbing the restaurant, Seymour just takes a dollar from each patron and claims that "I aim to go on a nonviolent spree and I need somebody who will fall in love with me along the way" (59).

The person who volunteers is a large, male Spokane Indian, whom Seymour calls "Salmon Boy" because the Spokanes are a salmon tribe. Although Seymour and Salmon Boy insist that they are not homosexual, as the journalist and the fighter did in "The Toughest Indian in the World," they become physically intimate because the narrative they are familiar with—outlaws on the run—dictates it.

> "Well, then, said, Salmon Boy." He asked, "Do you think we should kiss now?"
>
> "It seems like the right time, don't it?" asked Seymour. He licked his lips. (60)

Although he has no conscious goals or motivations, Seymour has internalized a set of rules and codes for appropriate behavior as an outlaw figure, claiming that they "need to terrorize an old man and his wife" (61). In reality, they end up just listening to her story about how her husband fought in the Second World War.

Seymour appears to be on a quest to understand human love and relationships, and in this story Alexie addresses the seeming deterioration of romantic love in contemporary society and the difficulties involved in male-male relationships of any kind. Seymour and Salmon Boy look for a love divorced from sex, cherishing physical intimacy without sex. Seymour tells Salmon Boy, "I think this is what women have wanted from men for all of our lives. I think they want to be held in our arms and fall asleep in the absence of body fluids" (70). Alexie suggests that, often unable to express emotion in ways other than through sex, men—not just Indian men but virtually all men—suffer interior emotional deficits by trying to adhere to the aggressive, emotionally undemonstrative, virile, male archetype. Salmon Boy later concludes, "It's a difficult thing for one man to love another man, whether they kiss each other or not" (73). By the end of the story, Seymour has changed to wanting to be "the Man Who Saved the Indian," but Alexie immediately undercuts this by stating that "he was a white man, and therefore he could dream" (74). Ultimately, Alexie describes them as "men in love with the idea of being in love" (74), reminiscent of Thomas Builds-the-Fire in Alexie's early story "Special Delivery," in which Thomas fought against crooked tribal cops with the idea of a gun. While Alexie does champion the imagination above virtually all else, it does not mean that he wants the reader to view these characters as sympathetic, for being in love with the idea of love is not being in love. It may be a positive first step or merely a delusion.

In a way, Alexie celebrates homosexuality as an alternative to male-dominated heterosexuality, suggesting that homosexuals are ultimately morally superior to most heterosexuals, especially heterosexual men, whom Alexie considers to be significantly more aggressive, violent, and destructive. In another story, "Indian Country," that addresses homosexuality, a male Indian mystery writer, Low Man Smith, encounters an old female friend, Tracy, a lesbian who once spurned him romantically. At the present time, Tracy is involved with an Indian woman, Sara Polatkin. When Low asks Sara why she has suddenly become a lesbian after previously being involved only with men, she responds: "I'm running away from the things of man" (139). To a large extent, this is also Alexie's purpose in the collection: to criticize codes of male behavior and what he perceives to be the hegemonic patriarchal system of Indian and mainstream American male culture.

By chance more than choice, Low Man becomes involved in the ensuing strife between Tracy, Sara, and Sara's devoutly religious parents, who disapprove of their daughter's relationship to the point of revulsion. It is Sara's parents, especially her dogmatic, pseudoreligious father, Sid, who are the targets for Alexie's (and Low's) scorn. Disgusted by their daughter's homosexuality, they label it as "sinful" (141). Low tries to dissuade Sid from his brash condemnation of homosexuality by questioning his moral and religious beliefs, suggesting that "Jesus was a fag. . . . Just think about it. I mean, there Jesus was, sticking up for the poor, the disadvantaged, the disabled. Who else but a fag would be that liberal, huh? And damn, Jesus hung out with twelve guys wearing great robes and great hair and never, ever talked about women. Tell me, Sidney, what kind of guys never talk about women?" (142). Low further says, "Jesus was an incredibly decent human being and they crucified him for it. He sounds like a fag to me" (143).

Low's comments suggest what Alexie ultimately argues in this and many other stories in the collection: that heterosexual (mainly white) men are the root of violence, degradation, and destruction. Indeed, as Low challenges Sid, Alexie puts women on a moral pedestal, suggesting that they are not prone to the same foibles as men. Alexie writes, "Sara looked at Low and wondered yet again why Indian men insisted on being warriors. *Put down your bows and arrows,* she wanted to scream at Low, at her father, at every hyper-masculine Injun in the world. *Put down your fucking guns and pick up your kids*" (144). Still, gender codes aren't completely responsible for the violence; the impoverished conditions on the reservation also contribute to the rage that helps produce the violence. As Low Man recalls of his own reservation life (at the Coeur d'Alene Reservation in Idaho), "The reservation's monotony might last months, sometimes years, before one man would eventually pull a pistol from a secret place and shoot another man in the face, or before a group of women would drag another woman out of her house and beat her left eye clean out of her skull" (122). That the story ends with Sid's attempted violent recapture of his daughter, his slapping of her, and attempted attack of Tracy shows how he is unable to communicate except through aggression and violence. That Sid fails and his daughter (Sara) and her lover (Tracy) leave shows that he is ultimately weaker and deficient in comparison to the two women. Because he lacks the ability to empathize and verbally communicate, Sid is ultimately responsible for the disintegration of the relationship between himself and his daughter.

Alexie's purpose is to deconstruct or demystify codes not only for Indian male authenticity but, more broadly, for all men. To be certain, there are few American icons as quintessentially masculine and American as John Wayne. At the same time, Wayne is often best known for playing rugged cowboys who are portrayed as heroes opposite the villainous, "savage" Indians whom he often battles. In "Dear John Wayne," Alexie turns the tables on Wayne by having a Spokane Indian woman, Etta Joseph, with whom Wayne had either an invented or an actual affair, tell the story. This hypothetical interview takes place in a retirement home in the year 2052 with the 118-year-old Etta who, despite her age, appears to have lost little or none of her mental acuity.

The arrogant white interviewer, an anthropology professor at Harvard and self-professed expert in mid- to late-twentieth-century Native American culture, is reminiscent of Clarence Mather in *Indian Killer*. The interviewer's book smarts about Native culture turn out to be ideas with little substance. For instance, during the interview, when the interviewer and Etta have a slight conflict, he describes it as "a tribal dialogue" that "solidifies familial and tribal ties" (193), when it is obvious that Etta does not even regard him, a white stranger, as being remotely tribal. Furthermore, he dehumanizes Etta when he says,

"I didn't recognize it as an integral and quite lovely component of the oral tradition. Of course, you had to insult me. It's your tradition." By suggesting that Etta is a cultural automaton without real free will, he takes away her agency. Etta calls the "knowledge" of the interviewer, gleaned from books often written by whites, "lies" that generalize and misrepresent Native culture.

Having read all the Western canonical masterpieces and having lived in the white world virtually all her life, Etta claims that she knows more about the white world than the questioner, who calls himself the leading scholar in his field, knows about Indian culture. Through Etta, Alexie claims that the firsthand, empirical knowledge that Etta possesses of the white world surpasses any secondhand accounts or theories derived from books, which is all the "knowledge" the interviewer ultimately possesses about Native culture. Etta tells him, "For the last one hundred and eighteen years, I have lived in your world, your white world. In order to survive, to thrive, I have to be white for fifty-seven minutes of every hour" (194).

One of Alexie's purposes is this story/interview is to tear down the illusion of John Wayne as a fearless, ultramasculine icon, which, according to Etta's account, is only an act. Etta portrays Wayne as a nervous and insecure sexual partner in this description of their lovemaking:

His hands were shaking, making it nearly impossible for him to properly fit the condom, so Etta Joseph reached down, smoothed the rubber with the palm of her left hand—she was touching John Wayne—and then guided him inside of her. He made love carefully, with an unintentional tantric rhythm: three shallow thrusts followed by one deep thrust, repeat as necessary. (196)

In fact, according to Etta's account, Wayne cries every time he has sex, and his tough, invulnerable, fearless demeanor is merely a sham. In despair he tells Etta, "Nobody knows me," and "John Wayne is the star. I'm Marion, I'm just Marion Morrison" (200). Later, when Wayne talks to his sons, he explains to them: "I have a public image to maintain. But that's not who I really am. I may act like a cowboy, I might pretend to be a cowboy, but I am not a cowboy in real life" (203). The uncertain, almost feminine Wayne/Morrison seeks shelter in the arms of Etta, whom Alexie or Etta portrays as being far stronger than Wayne/Morrison. Etta's Wayne is even afraid of horses, having been injured by one as a child.

Alexie has the male, iconic figure John Wayne express one of the main arguments in the collection, that "there's really not that much difference between men and women" (203). Furthermore, Alexie suggests that contemporary male identity is largely a self-perpetuating myth derived from unreal popular-culture icons like Wayne, whose archetypes are not only unrealizable but ultimately damaging to those who want to follow in their footsteps but fail to do so. In this story, it is Wayne, who, stereotypically, is purported to kill Indians only in self-defense or in the name of "justice," who falls desperately in love with one of the "enemy." In this story, Wayne calls up Etta on his deathbed, unable to speak to her (a sign of his poor communicative abilities) and weeping copiously, displaying his unrequited love for Etta. Alexie turns the tables on male, archetypal identity and on John Wayne and the western genre by having an Indian as the ultimate victor and survivor.

With "Dear John Wayne," Alexie seeks to counteract internalized feelings of marginalization and low self-worth experienced by many Indians, which produce individuals like the protagonist of the story "Class," Edgar, an urban Indian lawyer who has become comfortable with his perceived status as an accepted, lesser being in the white world. At parties, he claims that he would "always approach the tenth most attractive white woman at any gathering. I didn't have enough looks, charm, intelligence, or money to approach anybody more attractive than that, and I didn't have enough character to approach the less attractive" (38). Edgar has no real social consciousness or concern for the betterment of Indians; rather, he seeks only personal aggrandizement often through shameless use of his ethnicity. He informs the reader: "I'd been growing braids since I'd graduated from law school. My hair impressed jurors but irritated judges. Perfect" (39). Another example of his willful deception is the fact that he uses a phony Indian last name, "Eagle Runner," rather than his real last name, "Joseph," because of its perceived romanticism. Edgar's deception stems from his inner self-loathing, which his mother handed down to him. Edgar recalls, "She'd always wanted me to marry a white woman and beget half-breed children who would marry white people who would beget quarter-bloods, and so on and so on, until simple mathematics killed the Indian in us" (40). In fact, like his mother, who tells others she is of Spanish ancestry, Edgar often denies and misrepresents his ethnic identity to others.

Through these and other lies and misrepresentations, Edgar has grown emotionally deadened, evidenced by how he obsessively counts and details the exact number of parties, weddings, movies, and virtually every other activity he and his wife attend or engage in during their marriage. He knows his white wife is having an affair, but he does not confront her about it. Instead, he responds by having sex with prostitutes. Edgar, hungry for power over others, especially white people, insists on blue-eyed, blond-haired prostitutes, for procuring sex is for him essentially an attempt to counteract his own feelings of impotence toward whites.

That these prostitutes do not help Edgar achieve his desired power status becomes evident when he decides to stop using them after he switches from desiring a quintessentially European woman to an Indian woman, which the escort service he uses cannot provide. Although he never directly states it, Edgar seeks reconnection with his ethnic roots but isn't aware of how to go about doing it other than through sex and violence, which, according to Alexie, are the hallmarks of the heterosexual, mainstream American male. When sex fails, he frequents a tough, seedy, Indian bar, and while there, looking "like a Gap ad" (50), he is threatened by a lower-class, burly reservation Indian. Despite the fact that Edgar knows that this extremely strong man "could have killed me with the flick of his finger" (49), Edgar agrees to fight him in order to prove his manhood, or as Alexie explains it, "Deep in the heart of every Indian man's heart, he believes he is Crazy Horse" (53).

It comes as no surprise that Edgar is easily defeated and knocked unconscious. With aggression and violence failing him, Edgar returns to sex. While the Indian bartender, Sissy, tends to him, he makes a pass at her, which she immediately rejects. Presumably speaking for most women, she tells him, "Do you think I'm impressed by this fighting bullshit? Do you think it makes you some kind of warrior or something?" (55). The gulf between urban and reservation Indians, Alexie suggests, is huge, signified by how Sissy denies Edgar's claim that she and the others in the bar are his "people." Rather, Alexie suggests, economic class has become the larger determinant of identity. Edgar has the luxury of merely wanting a stronger identity, while most

Indians, like Sissy, are in stark financial straits, worrying "about having enough to eat" (56), and consequently often become violently jealous of others, like Edgar, who do not realize their own privileged positions.

Men are not the only ones drawn to the archetypal image of the savage, sexual Indian (typically male). The perceived sexual mystique of Indian men also draws an Indian woman, Mary Lynn, the protagonist of the story "Assimilation," into an adulterous affair. Married to a white man, Jeremiah, Mary Lynn appears in part to have become distrustful as a result of being Indian. The story begins with Mary Lynn's cynical, romantic perspective: "Regarding love, marriage, and sex, both Shakespeare and Sitting Bull knew the truth: treaties get broken. Therefore, Mary Lynn wanted to have sex with any man other than her husband" (1). In other words, Alexie suggests that as a result of Mary Lynn's mistrust, she plans an adulterous affair as a kind of preemptive strike against Jeremiah because she doesn't have faith in the institution of marriage. That Jeremiah has not cheated on her (although he has had a near affair), as it turns out, shows that Mary Lynn has become too mistrustful for her own good. Still, Jeremiah is in some ways mentally unfaithful to Mary Lynn, for Alexie reveals: "He was still in love with a white woman from high school he hadn't seen in decades. What Mary Lynn knew: he was truly in love with the idea of a white woman from a mythical high school, with a prom queen named *If Only* or a homecoming princess named *My Life Could Have Been Different*" (9).

Mary Lynn (and perhaps Alexie himself) anticipates the blame for her dissatisfaction as being based on ethnicity: "There were many people who would blame Mary Lynn's unhappiness, her dissatisfaction, on her ethnicity. God, she thought, how simple and earnest was that particular bit of psychotherapy" (2). Rather, Mary Lynn and Alexie would suggest that ethnicity is only one reason for her dissatisfaction. Some causes may be ethnically nonspecific, derived from the inherent difficulties involved in sustaining human relationships. However, to suggest that her unhappiness has nothing to do with her ethnicity doesn't make sense, considering Mary Lynn desires to sleep with an Indian man and that she "wanted to cheat on her white husband because he was white" (3). Presumably, it is Mary Lynn, not Alexie, who is unaware of this discrepancy. Mary Lynn proceeds to rationalize her behavior: "After all, she'd slept with a white stranger in her life, so why not include a Native American? Why not practice a carnal form of affirmative action? By God, her infidelity was a political act! Rebellion, resistance, revolution!" (4). Of course, one sexual act is hardly a revolution, but, like Edgar in "Class," it is through sexuality that Mary Lynn thinks she can rediscover or reconnect with her ethnic identity. Ultimately, it is a misguided attempt to recover her heritage and to communicate with another.

Ironically, in public, both Mary Lynn and her husband, Jeremiah, search for authenticity and ethnic stability when their own marriage inherently defies ethnic boundaries. When they eat at Tan Tan, a pan-Asian restaurant, Jeremiah tells her: "Don't you hate it when they have Chinese waiters in sushi joints? Or Korean dishwashers in a Thai noodle house?" (10). Furthermore, in their family, despite being interracial, race matters considerably more than in most noninterracial families. Their ethnically mixed progeny create internal problems between them. Their two daughters look mainly Caucasian while their two boys look mostly Indian, leading Mary Lynn's Indian parents to give their male grandchildren special treatment. In response to their unequal treatment, Jeremiah vows "to love the girls a little more than he loved the boys" (12). However, Jeremiah realizes that he may be rationalizing to cover up his preference for his Caucasian-looking daughters just as his in-laws do. "What if I love the girls more because they look more white than the boys?" he wonders. Similarly, Mary Lynn also may be biased with respect to her children's appearance. With two children who look mainly white and two who look mainly Indian, Mary Lynn concludes "that the genetic score was tied" (13). Furthermore, she tells Jeremiah, "We should have another kid, so we'll know if this is a white family or an Indian family." While this comment was presumably made in jest, it reveals how ethnicity or ethnic appearance ultimately rules this very divided family. Even Mary Lynn perceives a disequilibrium between herself and her husband on the basis of ethnicity. When Jeremiah responds, "It's a family family," Mary Lynn says, "Only a white guy would say that," indicating she believes that Jeremiah can't understand or comprehend ethnicity the way that she can since he does not belong to an ethnic minority. This, in a way, counteracts Mary Lynn's previous claim that her ethnic identity has little or nothing to do with her desire to sleep with an Indian man.

While both Mary Lynn and Jeremiah believe that race is "primarily a social construct," they also believe it legitimately exists, and their actions certainly demonstrate their belief in its existence. However, this story is not ultimately about the disintegration of a marriage and family, as it appears on the surface. Rather, the story suggests that changes can be made to re-cement bonds and change perspectives. For Jeremiah and Mary Lynn, it takes their observation of a tragedy in order to restore their connectedness. While on their way home from a restaurant, mere hours after Mary Lynn's affair, they get caught in a traffic jam caused by a white female poised to jump from a bridge. After Jeremiah leaves the car to inspect the cause, Mary Lynn hears a loud scream and becomes concerned that he might be endangered. She then has an epiphany: "Oh, God, she loved him, sometimes because he was white and often despite his whiteness. In her fear, she found one truth Sitting Bull never knew: there was at least one white man who could be trusted" (19). Likewise, Jeremiah comes to realize that "his wife was a constant." The story concludes with Jeremiah running back to Mary Lynn: "She and he loved each other across the distance" (20). That it takes a tragedy to produce an epiphany reveals that the cause of their problems may be their settled, middle-class existence. No longer having to really struggle for anything, they create problems for themselves, many of which are illusory. Still, Alexie leaves the reader with an ambiguous ending, which could mean that they will be able to bridge the distance between them or that they can only "love" each other from a distance (or because of the distance).

Alexie's sympathies lie mostly with Indians who hail from the reservation rather than those from urban areas, whom he often portrays as callous, self-absorbed, and immoral. Furthermore, Alexie seeks to overturn stereotypes of reservation dwellers as despondent, uneducated, often violent alcoholics. He does this in the story "Saint Junior," which focuses on the tough, resilient Fury couple. The "best basketball player his reservation has ever known" (153), Roman Gabriel Fury and his wife, Grace, live hermetic lives outside the reservation. Roman's self-enclosed world becomes apparent in his self-described political philosophy, which "revolved around the basic tenet that a person, any person, had only enough energy at any time to believe in three things. . . . Roman himself believed in free expression,

Grace Atwater [his wife], and basketball" (155). That Roman doesn't believe in his own ethnic heritage is not necessarily a deficiency in his or Grace's life, for their life is simple, but they, themselves, are far from being simple.

For Roman, a former international basketball player, basketball has become his main cultural heritage—one that breaks down arbitrary walls between people—rather than ethnicity, which creates boundaries. Alexie explains, "Roman knew that basketball was the most democratic sport. All you needed to play was something that resembled a ball and something else that approximated the shape of a basket" (156). At the same time, Alexie doesn't entirely glorify Roman's basketball playing, which is ultimately rather self-indulgent. Grace realizes that Roman plays basketball to "prove and test his masculinity" and that, "given the choice, he'd rather have been a buffalo hunter and soldier killer than the point guard for the Lakers, but there was no such choice, of course" (174–75). Roman is not a stereotypical ultra-athletic basketball player; he is well read and educated but has no desire to leave the reservation. Having traveled all around the world as an international basketball player, ultimately returning to the reservation with Grace after his early retirement, Roman is somewhere between an urban and reservation Indian, fitting in neither world. As Alexie explains, "Roman always felt like he didn't belong anywhere, like he couldn't belong to any one place or any series of places. Though his tribe had never been nomadic, he'd been born with the need to visit cities—every city!—where no Spokane Indian had ever been before" (159).

In contrast to the frequently destructive behavior on the reservation, Grace works as a fourth-grade teacher and as a stabilizing force in the lives of her often troubled students as well as a surrogate mother for them, as she and Roman have no children of their own. Despite her altruism, "Grace had never thought of herself as any kind of saint. More likely, she was just a good teacher, nothing wrong with that, but nothing uncommon or special about it either" (162). Even though the story is called "Saint Junior," Alexie does not try to sanctify these characters. They are a benevolent force on the reservation, but they are not saints. Still, their benevolence is a welcome alternative to the rampant anger and violence on the reservation. As Alexie describes, "Hell, these Spokanes started fist-fighting one another in the first grade and only stopped punching and kicking with the arrivals of their first Social Security checks."

Both Roman and Grace have the talent and intelligence to succeed in the white world, and they begin their lives showing exceptional promise, with both doing extremely well on their college entrance tests (Grace receiving a perfect score on hers). Yet from the very beginning, there are roadblocks along the way and people who doubt their intellectual abilities. For instance, after receiving excellent scores on his college entrance exam, Roman is called into the testing-service office in Spokane because they doubt his performance. Meanwhile, Grace attends St. Jerome the Second University (which she calls Saint Junior), but is dismayed at her largely snobby, white classmates, who often think she was admitted because of affirmative action.

Possibly in response to their experiences in the outside world, Grace and Roman return to the reservation, where they create a self-enclosed world; they are a community unto themselves, committed to "one basic truth: It was easy to make another person happy" (177). The two are able to do this and also more than survive. Throughout the years, Grace diligently writes poetry and fiction, publishing some in literary journals.

The story ends with a small press agreeing to publish an entire book of Grace's poetry and Roman returning to play basketball (albeit by himself) after a long hiatus. When Grace tells Roman, "this is a good life" (188), it is doubtful that Alexie feels otherwise. However, the somewhat enigmatic ending engenders some doubt. When shooting a basket, the ball "magically" catches on fire, "burn[ing] as it floated through the air." Once the burning ball comes to a stop on the ground, "Roman stepped toward his wife." The burning ball may signify the presence of a higher power in the lives of these two, but at the same time it may also show how basketball has created distance between them, a distance that can only really be bridged by its metaphoric destruction. The story ends with a single word, "Ceremony." However, it is unclear what activity denotes the ceremony. It may be basketball or it may be the relationship between Roman and Grace itself.

Similarly, Alexie tells a bittersweet but ultimately optimistic story about Indians in "One Good Man." Like most of the characters in *The Toughest Indian in the World,* the narrator is an Indian urbanite, a high-school English teacher in Spokane. While the narrator had planned to come back to the reservation after college, living outside of it has made him cognizant of what he believes to be its drawbacks: "As an adult, I am fully conscious of the reservation's weaknesses, its inherent limitations (geographic, social, economic, and spiritual), but as a child I'd believed the reservation to be an endless, magical place" (221). The narrator takes a leave of absence from school to care for his diabetic father, whose feet have been amputated and who doesn't have long to live.

Throughout the story, the narrator appears haunted by a question posed by one of his professors on his first day of class in his first year at Washington State University: *"What is an Indian?"* (224, italics in original). Throughout the story, the narrator offers his own answers to this question: *"What is an Indian?* Is it a son who can stand in a doorway and watch his father sleep?" (222). At other points in the story, the narrator wonders, "Is it a man with waiting experience, a man who can carry ten cups at the same time, one looped in the hook of each finger and both thumbs?" (235–36). Later he considers, "What is an Indian? Is it a man who can share his son and his wife?" (236).

As a kind of farewell gift, the narrator decides to take his father on a road trip to Mexico, but their van breaks down right before the border. Once again, the narrator ponders the same question but this time comes up with a different answer: *"What is an Indian?* I lifted my father and carried him across every border" (238). Ultimately, there is no exact definition of being "Indian," and with this ending Alexie suggests that self-sacrifice and family obligations outweigh ethnic identity. In its entirety, *The Toughest Indian in the World* shows significant development for Alexie as a writer who has gone beyond addressing merely ethnic concerns to examining the multilayered, inter-related problems of sexuality, economics, psychological identity, and family relations. Whereas in his earlier collections Alexie sometimes generalized about Indians, in this collection he is more content to leave the question *"What is an Indian?"* open to interpretation and as possibly unanswerable.

CHAPTER 8

Ten Little Indians

With his recent collection *Ten Little Indians* (2003), Alexie continues the exploration of urban Indians that he began with *The Toughest Indian in the World*. *Ten Little Indians* has much in common with *The Toughest Indian in the World:* an emphasis placed on sexuality, for instance, although not on homosexuality this time. However, the characters in *Ten Little Indians* are more comfortably situated between the Indian and white worlds. Whereas in *The Toughest Indian in the World* Alexie's characters tended to obsessively question the codes of Indian authenticity, in *Ten Little Indians* the major characters are less concerned with their ethnic identity. Being "Indian," while still important, is not the primary determinant of these characters' identities. This is not to suggest that Alexie or the characters themselves have found some happy medium between the reservation and city. Rather, most are socially isolated. However, their isolation is just as often caused by nonethnic reasons as ethnic reasons: poor family relations, psychological problems, and a patriarchal American culture.

By and large, the most sympathetic, motivated, and grounded characters in the stories are women. The first story, "The Search Engine," concerns Corliss, a nineteen-year-old sophomore at Washington State University. Alexie begins the story by creating a dichotomy between a white literary poser, who paraphrases famous writers in order to seduce women, and the humble but serious reader, Corliss, who is Indian. For the white man, literature, more specifically poetry, is only a means to an end, whereas for Corliss, who has a near obsession with literature, "the huge number of books confirmed how much magic she'd been denied for most of her life, and now she hungrily wanted to read every book on the shelf."[1] While Alexie's and the speaker's sympathies clearly lie with Corliss, she is less than saintly and unashamedly admits that "she judged people based on their surface appearances," justifying her actions with "Lord Byron said only shallow people don't judge by surfaces" (2). Furthermore, just as the young man uses literature as means to a personal end, Corliss has used her ethnicity as a means through with to receive favors, scholarships, and assistance. Alexie describes her as "a resourceful thief, a narcissistic Robin Hood who stole a rich education from white people and kept it," but he defends her actions: "For five centuries, Indians were slaughtered because they were Indians, so if Corliss received a free coffee now and again from the local free-range lesbian Indiophile, who could possibly find the wrong in that?" (5, 11).

Corliss has conflicted feelings about Indian/reservation culture, and rather than solely blaming mainstream American culture, as she had been taught to do while growing up on the reservation, Corliss also implicates Indians as being complicit in their economic and personal impoverishment due to their gradually accepted loss of self-sufficiency. Corliss seeks to transcend ethnic boundaries and refuses to always side with Indians over whites, reasoning that "it was easy to hate white vanity and white rage and white ignorance, but what about white compassion and white genius and white poetry?" (14). Rather, Corliss seeks to understand other cultures and break down ethnic boundaries, claiming at one point that she sometimes feels "like a white Jesuit priest" (15). Just as being Indian is not of supreme importance to Corliss, the problem she faces in embracing poetry in a culture that generally does not value it is not unique to Indians. Corliss has trouble understanding her father's and uncles' disdain of poetry, but she blames it more upon American standards for masculinity based upon physicality rather than solely blaming Indian culture. Caught between what she perceives as the unfounded romanticism of whites toward Indians and the defeated resignation of Indians, Corliss lives very much alone, fearing other Indians for their perceived codependency and avoiding other whites because she fears destroying their unrealizable chimeras about Indians. Not one to romanticize Indians or humanity for that matter, Corliss claims that "she never met one human being more interesting to her than a good book" (10).

Yet Corliss is forced to reconsider her avoidance of humanity with her discovery of a book of poems written by another Spokane Indian, Harlan Atwater, whose writings she implicitly believes can validate her intellectual pursuits, potentially help break her out of her self-imposed isolation, and also be a source of personal strength. Corliss, who believes herself to be the only real poetry reader on the Spokane Reservation, thinks she's found a kindred spirit in Atwater, whose poetry she thinks could be an alternative to the common mold of the reservation, embodied by Corliss's father and brothers, who mainly work in construction "not because they loved the good work or found it valuable or rewarding but because some teacher or guidance counselor once told them all they could work only blue-collar jobs" (13). While her intentions may be somewhat altruistic, Corliss is also motivated by her own personal desires. "Maybe this book could have saved her years of shame," she wonders. "Instead of trying to hide her poetry habit from her friends and family, and sneaking huge piles of poetry books into her room, maybe she could have proudly read a book of poems at the dinner table" (12).

Corliss, feeling herself to be on a "special mission" (25), ceaselessly searches for Atwater, eventually finding him in Seattle. Yet the extent to which Corliss has unfairly romanticized Atwater becomes clear in her first disappointed impression of him: "She'd hoped he would be an indigenous version of Harrison Ford. She'd wanted Indiana Jones and found Seattle Atwater" (33). That Atwater turns out to be a fraud, a Spokane Indian adopted by white people in Seattle who has no direct experience of the reservation, sheds some doubt on Corliss's acuity. For if she had in fact grown up on the same reservation as Atwater, she should have spotted inaccuracies in his poetry. Alexie suggests that out of her isolation and great desire to find another person like her, Corliss has deluded herself. She admits that she can be easily deceived by writers and by literature because of her deification of literature and writers. Atwater, who had fooled hundreds of people during his short apogee as a poet in the 1970s, has his own explanation for how he was able to maintain his identity masquerade: "Indian is easy to fake. People have been faking it for five hundred years. I was just better at it than most" (40). Indeed, if this is true, then it sheds doubt upon whether there is such a thing as true Indian authenticity (other than biological). In support of this idea, Alexie shows in a flashback how, during the height of his meager fame as a poet, Atwater was able to convince a large number of Indians, albeit drunk Indians, that he was Indian by reading his poetry. After reading his poetry, "he asked them if he was Indian, and they said he was the best Indian they'd ever known" (47). If Indians are indeed "obsessed with authenticity" (40), as Corliss claims, it may be a worthless obsession, given that ethnic authenticity itself is probably a chimera.

Her meeting with Atwater and her subsequent discovery of his fraudulent identity as a reservation Indian and of his brief life as a poet presumably has a significant impact upon Corliss. When she asks him for his real name, he leaves and she does not try to follow him. Rather, she waits in the bookstore where they talked for a few hours, probably reconsidering her ideas about herself and her definition of being "Indian." Then she "took Harlan Atwater's book to the poetry section, placed it with its front cover facing outward for all the world to see, and then she left the bookstore and began her small journey back home" (52). That she does this after discovering Atwater to be a fraud indicates she has come to believe that ethnic identity is not as important as the content of Atwater's poetry.

Whereas in *The Toughest Indian in the World* Alexie tended to lampoon and/or criticize urban, professional Indians, with the story "Lawyer's League" he creates a more admirable, part African American, part Indian man who has idealistic, political aspirations. This individual, Richard, points out an essential problem involved in achieving mainstream political power for Indians in that, more than other ethnic groups, Indians tend to mistrust politicians and that the political structures within Indian bureaucracies are often reverse meritocracies. Richard claims, "Quite a few of the state's most powerful Indian men and women are functionally illiterate. There are tribal councilmen who cannot spell the word 'sovereignty'" (54). The story concerns the inevitable problems this rather naive narrator faces in wanting to be "a good man and a great politician who makes promises and keeps them" (55). The implicit and explicit threat of racism daunts calculating Richard's ambitions. He rejects a possible relationship with a white woman because he fears future repercussions to his future political career: "I knew I would never achieve my full potential as a public servant if I married a white woman. I would lose votes each time I kissed my wife in public, and I would lose thousands of votes if my wise and terrible opponents create campaign ads that featured public displays of affection between my white wife and me" (61). Merely rejecting a white woman is not enough to remove the threat of racism, as Alexie reveals when Richard plays basketball with a group of white lawyers, one of whom, Bill, presumably threatened by Richard's basketball prowess, makes subtly racist comments, leading to a violent confrontation precipitated by Richard. The important message here is not only the violent act itself but the network of powerful whites that Richard cannot truly join. When Bill tells Richard they don't play Richard's "kind of ball" (65), he exposes a wide racial gulf that may doom Richard's political aspirations anyhow. Ever the calculating future politician, Richard is only concerned with whether or not he has tarnished his future political career. Mentally, he keeps rewriting his script, beginning with the unapologetic truth that punching Bill "felt good and true" to asking repentance from an imaginary audience (68). In the post-Clinton age of extreme personal scrutiny of political candidates and officeholders, Alexie suggests that obsessive calculation on the part of a future political candidate has become a necessity. However, a minority candidate has an increasingly difficult task in that he or she must try to deal civilly with the direct and indirect threats from the majority and at the same time not alienate the majority or the minority.

That many of the characters in *Ten Little Indians* are more generically American and less specifically Indian may in part be due to the fact that some, if not all, of the stories were written shortly after the events of September 11, 2001, which at least temporarily seemed to efface ethnicity in America. In the story "Can I Get a Witness?" a disgruntled, near-suicidal Spokane Indian woman/wife/mother survives a post-9/11 restaurant bombing in Seattle. The woman, who works as a paralegal, feels she is merely floating through her assigned roles in life as a mother, wife, and worker: "She was a parawife and a paramother and a parafriend" (71). The bombing helps jar her from her routine and provides her with an escape route from her dreary life. Later in the story, she admits that she was happy when she first saw the bomber because, "I knew I was going to survive. I was going to live, and I was going to crawl out of the ruins, and I was going to walk away from my life. I knew they'd never find me and would figure I was dead" (93). With the aftermath of the bombing, Alexie also makes some connections between violence and sexuality. The woman immediately thinks of having sex with a middle-aged white man who inquires after her. While she immediately labels herself "perverse" for having erotic thoughts, she then considers that it might be a "reflexive and natural reaction" (74). If her thoughts are abnormal and perverse, then her "perversity" may be a by-product of the media. Indeed, the woman recalls how her colleagues seemed to be erotically charged when they watched the twin towers collapse during 9/11. Therefore, she concludes, "We're so used to sex on TV that everything on TV becomes sexy, she thought" (88). It is more likely a natural reaction, however, and the woman offers some support for that theory with a half-in-jest proposition, but one that points to the importance of sexuality in virtually every human activity. Considering that most Islamic suicide bombers believe they will be rewarded in an afterlife with willing, submissive virgins, the woman concludes: "Political posturing aside, didn't a few thousand stupid men believe terrorism was another way to get laid? What would happen if the United States offered seventy-three virgins to each terrorist if he would abstain from violence? Instead of deploying an army of pissed-off U.S. soldiers to Afghanistan and Iraq, we could send a mercy team of patriotic virgins" (74). While this is hardly a realistic solution, it does identify how repressed sexuality may be a catalyst for terrorism, an idea rarely if ever discussed in contemporary society.

Still, this story is not so much about sexuality as it is a criticism of the post-9/11 atmosphere of American nationalism, which considered all victims to be saintly heroes, the country to be virtually without fault, and sparked a desire for retribution. The middle-aged man, a rather arrogant person whose ex-wife called him "Mr. Funny," for his constant joke telling, represents an archetypal American, too self-assured and materialistic. Alexie exposes his hidden faults with the fact that he was working on a computer game right before September 11, in which a person could play a terrorist who attacks American interests. After changing the game so that the players take the role of cops hunting terrorists (instead of vice versa), the game becomes hugely successful. The man suffers bouts of guilt due to his materialism, sometimes wondering "if he was a monster, making the games he made and earning the money he earned," (90). His extreme arrogance wins out, concluding that "I'm the highlight of every party. I'm the best dinner guest in the history of the world. I can make any woman fall in love with me in under five minutes and alienate her five minutes later."

Reacting against what she believes to be the "grief porn" of the post-9/11 media coverage, the woman insists that the attacks may not have been a complete tragedy in the sense that not all the victims were saintly and some, in fact, may have been despicable. Thereby, she argues that it is wrong to idealize all the victims of the attacks. She asks the man to consider that some "victims" might have been amoral and vicious individuals who physically abused their families and therefore "maybe . . . did deserve to die" (89). While the woman's reasoning doesn't in any way justify the actions of the terrorists, it does identify that there was a post-9/11 either/or dichotomy in America. One either completely grieved for all the victims and wholeheartedly supported the country or one was branded unpatriotic, a supporter of terrorism and Osama bin Laden. A person who tried to take a middle stance, like this woman, would have been considered by most to be in cahoots with the terrorists. This either/or dichotomy helped turn the woman's Indian husband and sons into flag-waving patriots and led her sons to want to be Marines, unaware or choosing to ignore that their purported love of America clashes with this country's treatment of Indians. The woman notes, "How could any Indian put on an U.S. military uniform and not die of toxic irony?" (91).

Furthermore, through the woman, Alexie also suggests that the roots of 9/11 may also be entrenched in the codes of male authenticity, stemming from the desire to prove one's superiority through aggression and violence. If the main culprit behind the terrorist attacks is masculinity, then the man, "Mr. Funny," suffers from deficiencies similar to those of the terrorists, except that he does not seek to prove his manhood through killing others but through saving, even loving, the woman. Furthermore, the man's huge, unfounded self-confidence and arrogance are dangerous in the sense that he perceives himself to be better than virtually everyone else. "He wanted his love to be different than everybody else's," Alexie writes. "He wanted his love to be the only true image of God. He wanted his love to be the tyrant that saved the world no matter if the world desired to be saved" (95). Still, his encounter with the woman helps change his perspective. When he goes outside with the woman, instead of seeing benevolent passersby, he imagines the horrific secrets each holds: "He knew that man cheated on his wife with her sister and that woman pinched her Alzheimered mother's arms until they bled. And that teenage boy set dogs on fire and that pretty teenaged girl once knocked down a fat ugly girl and spit in her mouth" (94). The man finally concludes, "We're all failures" (95). Due to his revelation, the man begins to shed his arrogant, ultraconfident facade, evidenced by the fact that he no longer feels that he can save the woman but that if he loves the woman "he might be saved." The fact that he lets the woman go after she breaks away from him also shows a newfound resignation in his character.

While they don't play as large a role in "Can I Get a Witness?" the events of 9/11 also play an important role in the story "Flight Patterns," in that they help create bonds between people of different ethnicities while also emphasizing the importance of family and love. For Alexie, family is the main thing that saves people, especially men, from succumbing to what he believes to be their underlying violent tendencies. The main character of "Flight Patterns," William, a successful urban Indian executive, husband, and father, reveals his subverted violent tendencies in his dreams:

When he traveled, he had nightmares about strangers breaking in to his house and killing and raping Marie and Grace. In other nightmares, he arrived home in time to save his family by beating the intruders and chasing them away. During longer business trips, William's nightmares became more violent as the days and nights passed. If he was gone over a week,

he dreamed about mutilating the rapists and eating them alive
while his wife and daughter cheered for him. (110)

William tells Fedaku, an Ethiopian taxi driver who takes him to
the airport, how much he loves his family: "Sometimes I worry
their love is the only thing that makes me human, you know? I
think if they stopped loving me, I might burn up, spontaneously
combust, and turn into little pieces of oxygen and hydrogen and
carbon" (113). William's overwhelming belief in love and family is undermined when he talks to Fedaku, who tells him how
he fled his native country, Ethiopia, after he refused to continue
bombing insurgent groups. In consequence, he can no longer see
his family in Ethiopia and doubts he ever will again. Fedaku
does not "spontaneously combust," as William claims he would,
which suggests that William uses his family as something of a
crutch. While William can't be certain if Fedaku has told him
the truth, it ultimately doesn't matter. "William was convinced,"
Alexie explains, "that somewhere in the world, somewhere in
Africa or the United States, a man, a jet pilot, wanted to fly away
from the war he was supposed to fight. There must be hundreds,
perhaps thousands of such men, and how many were coura-
geous enough to fly away?" (121). Talking to Fedaku inspires
William with love for his family, and he rushes to call them from
the airport. The story ends with him telling his wife, "I'm here,"
signifying that he has come to fully appreciate how lucky he is,
whereas before meeting Fedaku, he considered his family to be
"special" and, in a way, better than others (110).

The characters in *Ten Little Indians* are often complex, not
always completely sympathetic, and often equally influenced if
not more influenced by American popular culture than their own
ethnicity. For instance, Estelle, in the story "The Life and Times
of Estelle Walks Above," is a single mother who is largely shaped

by receiving a poor score on a parenting quiz in popular magazine, which gets her to take an almost obsessive interest in her son's life and leads her to embrace the burgeoning feminist movement during the 1970s. As the narrator explains, "Despite her roving and restless intelligence, my mother was the kind of person who believed the garbage she read in magazines" (127). This is not to suggest that the narrator, Estelle's son, believes the feminist movement to be garbage, but he is befuddled by his mother's new treatment of him as a peer, not a teenaged son, to the point that she insists that he come with her to her feminist meetings and gives him sex advice.

In truth, Estelle may be drawn to the feminist movement because, within the movement, other white women look up to her because she is an Indian woman. She is not able to secure as much power in any Indian community. The narrator explains: "I don't think every white person I meet has the spiritual talents and service commitment of a Jesuit priest, but white folks often think we Indians are shamanic geniuses" (139). That Estelle seeks to capitalize on her Indian heritage can be seen in how she uses a false Indian name, Walks Above, rather than her real but generic last name, Miller. The narrator even suggests that his mother (and, to some extent, he himself as well) is guilty of hypocrisy in her attitude toward white people, whom she often castigates without acknowledging that her livelihood and good fortune has typically depended upon their goodwill: "My mother went to college on scholarships funded by white people; she was a teaching assistant to a white professor; she borrowed money from white people who didn't have much money to lend; our white landlord let us pay half rent for a whole year and never asked for the rest; my favorite baby-sitter was a white woman with red hair" (139). Furthermore, the narrator explains that most of his mother's and his own friends are white, concluding that they are both "hostages of colonial contradictions" (140).

Still, the story is more a celebration of femininity, and the male narrator considers himself to be mostly inadequate in the context of the other women in his life, at one point claiming that "smart women surround me and lovingly tolerate my stupidity" (142). He also criticizes Indian men for trying to adhere to false standards of authenticity: "I love the way Indian men wear their hair long, cry too easily, wear florid clothes—all reds and pinks and lavenders and turquoises—and sing and dance most every day of their lives. If you think about it, Indian men are probably the most feminized males on the planet (and I mean that as a compliment), despite how ridiculously macho we pretend to be" (135).

The story concludes with the narrator and his mother spotting a woman who has a menstrual stain on her dress. The difference in male and female response is particularly telling: "Some of the men and boys laughed and pointed," while "an older woman ran a red light, steered her car across three lanes of traffic, and braked to a stop halfway onto the sidewalk. She exploded out of her car with a coat in her hands, wrapped it around the waist of the woman in the white dress, and rushed back to the car" (149). This affects the narrator and Estelle to the extent that the narrator screams to Estelle to "do something," which leads her to scream and slap him. The story ends with the simple message of the importance of family, despite its imperfections: "My mother and I have loved and failed each other, and we keep on loving and failing each other, and one of us will eventually bury the other, and the survivor will burn down the church with grief's hungry fire."

With the story "Do You Know Where I Am?" Alexie also investigates the inner workings of relationships and concludes that they are largely built upon trust. The main characters are two smitten Indian college students who experience an event that disturbs their relationship. After they rescue a cat and return it to its proper owners, the man, David, lies and tells the couple that it was he who remembered their ad (it was actually his future wife, Sharon) and takes the reward money. This one event comes to shape Sharon's conception of David, and although, after a long separation, she agrees to marry him, she tells David, "You're a liar. I'm going to marry a liar" (158). Throughout their marriage, "All during those years, at every house part, group dinner, family gathering, and company picnic, Sharon told the story of the lost cat. 'My husband, the liar,' she always called me" (159). Although she never explains it as such, this breach of trust may lead to Sharon's brief extramarital affair, which she tells David about ten years into their marriage. With this adulterous act, Alexie also reverses stereotypical gender roles, with the faithful man being stung by his wife's infidelity. That race matters immensely to David becomes clear in his exuberance that Sharon slept with a white man rather than an Indian man: "Call it a potent mix of arrogance and self-hatred, but I was certain I was the one Indian man who was good enough for my Indian wife" (162). Curiously, it doesn't seem to affect David that much, claiming they "formally rebuilt our marriage. And it was blue-collar work, exhausting and painful. We didn't argue more often than before, but we did live with longer and greater silences" (166). Like the narrator in "The Life and Times of Estelle Walks Above," David is a good-hearted but mostly somnolent man, who loves but is distant from his family. Most tellingly, for his fortieth birthday, Sharon and their kids get him "a T-shirt that read LOST CAT on the front and DO YOU KNOW WHERE I AM? on the back." Not only does the shirt show how important the initial event still is to Sharon, it also points how oblivious David has become. He, in essence, has become the lost cat. The final scene of the story, several decades later, finds Sharon dying of cancer and David at her bedside, telling her that "I would fistfight Time to win back your youth" (168). Still harping on the incident with the cat decades earlier, she responds, "You're a liar," to which David insists that he lied to her "only once." It is impossible to determine whether David is being honest or not, but for Sharon at least, one breach of trust is enough to shape her impression of him.

Whereas most of the characters in *Ten Little Indians* are urban professionals, the main character, Jackson Jackson, in "What You Pawn I Will Redeem" is a homeless, Spokane Indian alcoholic who lives in Seattle. Jackson, although certainly troubled, is far from defeated and goes on a mission to recover his grandmother's fancydancing regalia, which he discovers in a pawnshop. The pawnbroker initially agrees to sell it to Jackson if he can come up with the thousand dollars that it cost the pawnbroker to buy it. The extent to which family is important to this character is apparent in his monomaniacal, twenty-four-hour hapless pursuit of the money. He insists, "I know it's crazy, but I wondered if I could bring my grandmother back to life if I bought back her regalia" (176). The good-hearted Jackson does scrounge together some money, but ends up spending most of it on alcohol and food for other hungry and alcoholic Indians. When he comes back to the pawnshop, however, it is the white pawnbroker who selflessly gives him the fancydancing regalia for free. The narrator concludes, "Do you know how many good men live in the world? Too many to count!" (194). The narrator "redeems" himself by taking the regalia and dancing it in the street, with the narrator concluding, "I was my grandmother, dancing." This story is a first for Alexie, in which a white man is ultimately the hero of the story, suggesting that Alexie's perspective toward non-Natives may have softened.

Ten Little Indians concludes with a story, "What Ever Happened to Frank Snake Church?" about the long, gradual transformation of a former Indian basketball star called Frank Snake Church. Frank is rather misguided by his conceptions of Indian traditions and is happily ensconced in a dependent relationship with his parents, who are his only real connections to the social world. Following Frank's completion of high school, his mother dies, and "to honor her and keep her memory sacred, Frank knew he had to give up something valuable" (202), so he decides to forsake his basketball scholarship. In truth, however, Frank is more of a masochist, seeking more to punish himself than he seeks to commemorate his mother, as it is dubious at best how giving up his basketball scholarship at the University of Washington in any way commemorates his mother.

The only time that Frank believes that he has an authentic "Indian" vision is while hiking, when he thinks his father has died, which is actually a manifestation of his greatest fear. While his "vision" proves to be inaccurate on this occasion, his father does die a year later. When his father dies, at first Frank completely deteriorates mentally to the point that when cleaning out his father's house, he literally consumes the hair of his father that he finds lingering in his comb, in his sheets, and elsewhere. It takes the loss of his father to force painful truths upon Frank, who comes to the realization that his desire for solitude and isolation, his dreams of being the last person alive after an epidemic or mass holocaust, smacks of "arrogance and misanthropy"

(205). Alexie describes Frank's gradual revelation: "All along, Frank understood that he was suffering from a quiet sickness, a sort of emotional tumor that never grew or diminished but prevented him from living a full and messy life. At the end of every day, Frank thoroughly washed away the human funk of the world, but now, with his father's death, he worried that he would never feel clean again."

Frank replaces his familial dependence with an exercise addiction. Indeed, when Frank goes to enlist the help of an athletic trainer, Russell, "Russell could feel Frank's desperation and sense of purpose, the religious fervor that needed to be directed. Russell had met a thousand desperate people, all looking to rescue or be rescued, but this Indian man was especially radiant with need" (207). While such dependence is physically healthy, it does little to improve Frank's mental instability. Indeed, Frank misguidedly insists that, through his exercise program, he will be able to "drown" death "before you drown me" (209). Yet, in a way, Frank is already socially deadened. Although he completely refurbishes his home during this transformative period, he also refuses all visitors and cuts off the phone. Even Frank realizes his underlying problems run deeper: "Frank knew his behavior was obsessive and compulsive, and perhaps he was seriously disturbed, in need of medical care and strong prescriptions, but he didn't want to stop. He needed to perform this ceremony, to disappear into the ritual, to methodically change into something new and better, into someone stronger" (210).

In order to transform into something better or at least into what he perceives as better, Frank begins playing basketball. In virtually all his work up to this point, Alexie had nearly always extolled the benefits of basketball, but in this story basketball is just another crutch or compulsive addiction for Frank, an opportunity for him to falsely prove his manhood and feel superior to others. In describing basketball, Alexie is ambivalent, pointing out its drawbacks as well as its benefits: "In basketball, there is no such thing as 'too much' or 'too far' or 'too high.' In basketball, enough is never enough. At its best and worst, basketball is all about excess. Every day is Fat Tuesday on a basketball court" (214). It is only when another basketball player, nicknamed The Preacher, verbally accosts Frank that Frank comes to his senses. The Preacher questions why Frank is playing: "You're not some sixteen-year-old gangster trying to play your way out of the ghetto. You ain't even some reservation warrior boy trying to shoot your way off the reservation and into some white-collar job at Microsoft Ice Cream. You're just Frank the Pretty Good Shooter for an Old Fart" (226). Frank claims he plays to remember his mother and father, but the preacher claims he's just playing to "remember yourself" (228). Indeed, basketball for Frank is an indulgence, a compulsive addiction, and a diversion from social life. When The Preacher tells him, "You're just an old fart dying of terminal nostalgia," Frank subconsciously realizes how he has largely created his own misguided, self-imposed isolation and misery. Subsequently, he falls into a suicidal withdrawal, saved only by his athletic trainer, Russell, who comes to his rescue.

After a year of treatment, Frank is able to discard all his compulsive addictions and crutches and decides to enroll in college at West Seattle Community College at the age of forty-one. This is where Frank courageously finally faces his fears, even though it was "his therapist who had suggested it" (233). All throughout the application process, Frank feels inadequate but proceeds on. During his first semester, seeking his old familiar crutch, he plays a practice game with the basketball team.

During this game, Frank severely injuries his knee, presumably to the point that he will never play basketball competitively again, but Alexie takes this seemingly devastating ending and makes it uplifting. When the point guard tells Frank that he's going to be fine, Frank responds, "I know" (243), which suggests that Frank has finally conquered his compulsive addictions (including basketball) and has found or is on his way to finding a real, interior strength. No longer burdened by the Indian warrior archetype, Frank has become more of what Alexie would describe as a genuine male archetype for Indians (and presumably for all Americans): secure enough to admit vulnerabilities and to develop a nonaggressive, individual identity.

That being Indian doesn't factor much into this and many of the other stories in *Ten Little Indians* shows that the title of the collection is something of a misnomer. Rather, most of Alexie's characters in the collection, Indian though they may be, exist in a kind of limbo, suspended between mainstream American and Indian conceptions and identities. They may be described as being somewhat postethnic. To be sure, throughout his career, Alexie has mainly focused upon Indians and has expressed no desire to do otherwise. Still, this collection evinces an Alexie who has gradually transformed from writing almost solely about ethnicity to writing more about generic, human, or American issues of family, relationships, individual and collective identity, politics, and morality. He has come a long way, both personally and literarily, from his beginnings on the Spokane Indian Reservation, but not so far that he has forgotten his ethnic and personal roots.

Notes

Chapter 1—Understanding Sherman Alexie

1. Quoted in Tomson Highway's on-line interview, "Spokane Words," *Aboriginal Voices,* January–March 1997, http://www.falls apart.com/art-av.html (accessed March 2003).

2. Quoted in Highway, "Spokane Words."

3. Lynn Cline, "About Sherman Alexie," *Ploughshares* 26, no. 4 (Winter 2000/2001): 197.

4. Quoted in Georgia Pabst's article "Alexie Sends Strong Signals," *Milwaukee Journal Sentinel,* March 9, 2002, http://www.jsonline.com/enter/books/mar02/25632.asp (accessed April 2003).

5. Quoted in Juliette Torrez's on-line interview, "Juliette Torrez Goes Long Distance with Sherman Alexie," *(Sic) Vice & Verse,* August 31, 1999. Available at http://poetry.about.com/library/weekly/aa083199.htm?once=true&terms=alexia (accessed April 2003).

6. Quoted in Cline, "About Sherman Alexie," 199.

7. Quoted in Highway, "Spokane Words."

8. This is not to suggest that Alexie is only interested and influenced by Native writers. Many of his favorite writers and literary influences are non-Natives. As he explains: "Walt Whitman and Emily Dickinson are two of my favorites. Wallace Stevens leaves me kind of dry, but the other poets, they're still a primary influence. I always tell people my literary influences are Stephen King, John Steinbeck, and my mother, my grandfather and the Brady Bunch." Quoted in Highway, "Spokane Words."

9. For Alexie, this is a watershed moment in his life. As he recalls, "I loved alcohol the most, loved it more than anybody or anything. That's what I wrote about. And it certainly accounted for some great writing. But it accounted for two or three years of good writing—it would never account for 20 years of good writing. I would have turned into Charles Bukowski. He wrote 10,000 poems

and 10 of them were great." Quoted in Joelle Fraser, "Sherman Alexie's *Iowa Review* Interview," http://www.english.uiuc.edu/maps/poets/a_f/alexie/fraser.htm (accessed March 2003).

10. Quoted in Highway, "Spokane Words."

11. Quoted in Highway, "Spokane Words."

12. Quoted in Fraser, "Sherman Alexie's *Iowa Review* Interview."

13. Sherman Alexie, "Making Smoke," *Whole Earth* 94, no. 1 (Fall 1998): 102–3.

14. Quoted in *Sidewalk*'s on-line interview with Sherman Alexie (1999). Available at http://www.fallsapart.com/art-side.html (accessed March 2003).

15. Quoted in Duncan Campbell's on-line interview, "Voices of the New Tribe," *Guardian* (Manchester), January 4, 2003, http://books.guardian.co.uk/review/story/0,12084,868123,00.html (accessed March 2003).

16. Quoted in Campbell, "Voices of the New Tribe."

17. Quoted in Joel McNally, "Sherman Alexie," *Writer* 114, no. 6 (June 2001): 30.

18. In an interview, Alexie further explains his reasoning: "In order for the Indian kid to read me, pop culture is where I should be. Literary fiction is very elitist. The fifteen or twenty thousand literary-book buyers in this country, I'm very happy for them, and I'm happy they buy my books, by and large. But there is a whole other population out there I want to reach. And so for me, what kind of art can I create that gets to them? I don't want to have an elitist career. I've won awards, I've gotten a lot of attention, I've been in *The New Yorker*, I'm very happy with all that. I'm very proud. But I would consider myself a failure if more people didn't read me. I'd rather be accessible than win a MacArthur." Quoted in Russ Spencer, "What It Means to Be Sherman Alexie," *Book Magazine,* July/August 2000, http://www.bookmagazine.com/archive/issue11/alexie.shtml (accessed April 2003).

19. Quoted in Fraser, "Sherman Alexie's *Iowa Review* Interview."

20. Quoted in Fraser, "Sherman Alexie's *Iowa Review* Interview."

21. Quoted in Cline, "About Sherman Alexie," 199.

22. Sherman Alexie, "Death in Hollywood," *Ploughshares* 26, no. 4 (Winter 2000/2001): 8–9.

23. Quoted in McNally, "Sherman Alexie," 30.

24. Quoted in Jessica Chapel, "Interview with Sherman Alexie," *Atlantic Online,* June 1, 2000, http://www.theatlantic.com/unbound/interviews/ba2000-06-01.htm (accessed March 2003).

25. Quoted in Fraser, "Sherman Alexie's *Iowa Review* Interview."

26. Quoted in *Sidewalk*'s on-line interview with Sherman Alexie (1999).

27. Granted, it is commonly accepted that Native Americans entered North America during the Ice Age, across the frozen Bering Strait, approximately twenty-five thousand to thirty thousand years ago.

28. Andrew Macdonald, Gina Macdonald, and MaryAnn Sheridan, *Shape-Shifting: Images of Native Americans in Recent Popular Fiction* (Westport, Conn.: Greenwood Press, 2000), xi.

29. William Bevis, "Native American Novels: Homing In," in *Critical Perspectives on Native American Fiction,* ed. Richard Fleck (Washington, D.C.: Three Continents Press, 1993), 31.

30. See Jace Weaver, *That the People Might Live: Native American Literatures and Native American Community* (New York: Oxford University Press, 1997).

31. See Bonnie Duran, Eduardo Duran, and Maria Yellow Horse Brave Heart, "Native Americans and the Trauma of History," in *Studying Native America,* ed. Russell Thornton (Madison: University of Wisconsin Press, 1998).

32. Weaver, *That the People Might Live,* 11.

33. Russell Thornton, "The Demography of Colonialism and 'Old' and 'New' Native Americans," in *Studying Native America,* 30.

34. Norma Wilson, *The Nature of Native American Poetry* (Albuquerque: University of New Mexico Press, 2001), 1.

35. Bevis, "Native American Novels," 28.

36. Bevis, "Native American Novels," 28.

37. James Ruppert, "Mediation in Contemporary Native American Writing," in *Native American Perspectives on Literature and History,* ed. Alan R. Velie (Norman: University of Oklahoma Press, 1995), 128.

38. Alan R. Velie, "The Trickster Novel," in *Narrative Chance: Postmodern Discourse on Native American Indian Literatures,* ed. Gerald Vizenor (Norman: University of Oklahoma Press, 1993), 122.

39. Gerald Vizenor, "Trickster Discourse: Comic Holotropes and Language Games," in *Narrative Chance,* 188.

40. Weaver, *That the People Might Live,* 26.

41. As Norma Wilson describes, "The first books of N. Scott Momaday, Leslie Marmon Silko, James Welch, Linda Hogan, and Louise Erdrich were collections of poems, and although the reading public is better acquainted with their novels, all five of these authors are accomplished poets" (Wilson, *Nature,* 1).

42. Wilson also argues that there are "definite parallels between the poetry of the English Romantics, particularly William Blake, and Native American poetry. The English Romantics' celebration of nature, their recognition of particular birds as symbols of freedom and spirit, and their emphasis on spirituality, along with their condemnation of industry's pollution and destruction of the natural environment and rural life, are literary precedents of contemporary indigenous poetry" (Wilson, *Nature,* 3).

43. Wilson, *Nature,* 11.

44. Raymond Fogelson, "Perspectives on Native American Identity," in *Studying Native America,* 48.

45. See Shari Huhndorf, *Going Native: Indians in the American Cultural Imagination* (Ithaca, N.Y.: Cornell University Press, 2001), 166; and Lois Einhorn, *The Native American Oral Tradition: Voices of Spirit and Soul* (Westport, Conn.: Praeger, 2000), 15. Furthermore, Einhorn argues, "One of the most important ways the assumptions of Native People differ from those of their non-Native

counterparts is their focus on the circle. 'Civilized' human beings represent the first living species to measure time in a linear manner. All other life forms deal with the continual ebbs and flows of circular energies. Like those other life forms, Native Americans maintain an intimate relationship with the sun and the moon—circular, primal forms" (15).

46. Raymond DeMallie, "Kinship: The Foundation for Native American Society," in *Studying Native America,* 306.

47. Thomas King, a Cherokee, declares the "most important relationship . . . is embodied within the idea of community. Community, in a Native sense, is not simply a place or a group of people, rather it is, as novelist Louise Erdrich describes it, a place that has been 'inhabited for generations' where 'the landscape becomes enlivened by a sense of group and family history.'" Quoted in *All My Relations: An Anthology of Contemporary Canadian Native Fiction,* ed. Thomas King (Norman: University of Oklahoma Press, 1992), xiii–xiv.

48. Weaver, *That the People Might Live,* 43.

49. Quoted in Campbell, "Voices of the New Tribe."

50. Macdonald, Macdonald, and Sheridan, *Shape-Shifting,* 246.

51. Quoted in Cline, "About Sherman Alexie," 31.

Chapter 2—*The Business of Fancydancing* and *Old Shirts and New Skins*

1. Leslie Ullmann, "Betrayals and Boundaries: A Question of Balance," *Kenyon Review* 15, no. 3 (Summer 1993): 183.

2. Sherman Alexie, *The Business of Fancydancing* (Brooklyn, N.Y.: Hanging Loose Press, 1992), 69. Further references to this book are noted parenthetically in the text.

3. Diane Niatum, "History, Nature, Family, Dream: The Musical Colors of their Poems," in *Looking at the Words of Our People,* ed. Jeannette Armstrong (Penticton, British Columbia: Theytus Books, 1993), 66.

4. Einhorn, *Native American Oral Tradition,* 3.

5. Quoted in "New Perspectives on the West," *PBS—The West.* Available at http://www.pbs.org/weta/thewest/people/a_c/buffalobill .htm (accessed May 2003).

6. Sherman Alexie, *Old Shirts and New Skins* (Los Angeles: American Indian Studies Center, University of California, Los Angeles, 1993), 76. Further references to this book are noted parenthetically in the text.

Chapter 3—*First Indian on the Moon* and *The Lone Ranger and Tonto Fistfight in Heaven*

1. Sherman Alexie. *First Indian on the Moon* (Brooklyn, N.Y.: Hanging Loose Press, 1993), 9. Further references to this book are noted parenthetically in the text.

2. Denise Low, review of *The Lone Ranger and Tonto Fistfight in Heaven, American Indian Quarterly* 20, no. 1 (Winter 1996): 123.

3. James Cox, "Muting White Noise: The Subversion of Popular Culture Narratives of Conquest in Sherman Alexie's Fiction," *Studies in American Indian Literature* 9, no. 4 (Winter 1997): 56.

4. Cox, "Muting White Noise," 56.

5. Sherman Alexie, *The Lone Ranger and Tonto Fistfight in Heaven* (New York: Atlantic Monthly Press, 1993), 1. Further references to this book are noted parenthetically in the text.

6. Velie, "The Trickster Novel," 408.

Chapter 4—*Reservation Blues*

1. Quoted in Highway, "Spokane Words."

2. Quoted in Highway, "Spokane Words."

3. Sherman Alexie, *Reservation Blues* (New York: Warner Books, 1995), 114. Further references are noted parenthetically in the text.

4. Bobby Lake-Thom, *Spirits of the Earth: A Guide to Native American Nature Symbols, Stories, and Ceremonies* (New York: Plume, 1997), 155.

5. Peter Aschoff, "The Poetry of the Blues: Understanding the Blues in Its Cultural Context," in *The Triumph of the Soul* (Westport, Conn.: Praeger, 2001), 36.

6. Ralph Ellison, *Shadow and Act* (New York: Vintage International, 1995), 3.

7. Aschoff claims, "Unlike Christianity, which teaches that, at the time of death, the human soul leaves for Heaven or Hell and ceases to be a part of this world, West African animists like the Kongo believe that the ancestral spirit remains a very real part of this world and thus must be dealt with as one would deal with any other member of one's family and society" (55).

8. Jon Michael Spencer, *Blues and Evil* (Knoxville: University of Tennessee Press, 1993), 7.

9. Karen Jorgensen, "White Shadows: The Use of Doppelgangers in Sherman Alexie's *Reservation Blues*," *Studies in American Indian Literature* 9, no. 4 (Winter 1997): 54.

10. Jorgensen, "White Shadows," 55.

11. It is unclear whether Alexie used a real historical event for the basis of Junior's dream, but it is safe to assume that this kind of event happened on more than one occasion during the settlement of the West.

12. Later in the novel, Father Arnold is convinced to stay by his religious superior, who tells Arnold that there is no one else who can replace him.

Chapter 5—*Indian Killer*

1. Quoted in Fraser, "Sherman Alexie's *Iowa Review* Interview."

2. Quoted in Cline, "About Sherman Alexie," 201.

3. Quoted in Campbell, "Voices of the New Tribe."

4. Quoted in Campbell, "Voices of the New Tribe."

5. Quoted in Campbell, "Voices of the New Tribe."

6. John Skow, "Lost Heritage," *Time* 148, no. 19 (October 21, 1996): 88.

7. By naming the killer John Smith, Alexie probably refers to the original colonist and writer, John Smith, who was among the first settlers in Virginia and was abducted by Native Americans. Smith describes his encounters with Native Americans in *A General History* (1624). In a sense, the original John Smith was the first powerful, European colonizer in the New World.

8. Quoted in Highway, "Spokane Words."

9. Duran, Duran, and Brave Heart, "Native Americans and the Trauma of History," 69.

10. Sherman Alexie, *Indian Killer* (New York: Warner Books, 1996), 114. Further references to this book are noted parenthetically in the text.

11. Ron McFarland, "Sherman Alexie's Polemic Stories," *Studies in American Indian Literature* 9, no. 4 (Winter 1997): 34.

12. Lake-Thom, *Spirits of the Earth,* 117.

13. In an interview, Alexie further explains his criticism of some of these works: "The same man who wrote that book [*Lakota Woman*] also wrote *Lame Deer, Seeker of Visions*. Once again, these autobiographies are not really autobiographies, they're translations. Both writers of those books have freely admitted to poetic license. Poetic license and manifest destiny are often the same thing" (quoted in "Spokane Words"). Alexie's claim about *The Education of Little Tree* has been substantiated; see Tom Gliatto's article *"The Education of Little Tree"* in *People Weekly* 37, no. 22 (December 15, 1997): 87–92; or Michael Marker's *"The Education of Little Tree: What It Really Reveals about the Public Schools,"* in *Phi Delta Kappan* 74, no. 3 (November 1992). There is more dissent about *Black Elk Speaks,* with prominent Indian activist Vine Deloria Jr. calling it "a North American Bible for all tribes" (quoted in Carl Silvio, "*Black Elk Speaks* and Literary Disciplinarity: A Case Study in Canonization," *College Literature* 26, no. 2 [Spring 1999]: 138) while others, like Alexie, question the authenticity of the text. For a history of the academic disputes surrounding *Black Elk Speaks,* see Silvio's article. While it is true that a white man (Richard Erdoes) co-wrote

or co-edited *Lakota Woman* and *Lame Deer: Seeker of Visions,* it is not clear how much power he had in shaping the novel or whether his influence perverted the actual content.

14. For more information about the Ghost Dance, see Macdonald, Macdonald, and Sheridan's *Shape-Shifting.*

Chapter 6—*The Summer of Black Widows* and *One Stick Song*

1. Sherman Alexie, *The Summer of Black Widows* (Brooklyn, N.Y.: Hanging Loose Press, 1996), 3. Further references to this book are noted parenthetically in the text.

2. Lake-Thom, *Spirits of the Earth,* 84.

3. See Vine Deloria Jr.'s essay "Sacred Places and Moral Responsibilities," in *The Great Plains,* ed. Deborah Carmichael et al. (Fort Worth, Tex.: Harcourt Custom, 2001).

4. Donna Seaman, "Read-alikes: Contemporary Native American Fiction," *Booklist* 97, no. 8 (December 15, 2000): 787.

5. Sherman Alexie, *One Stick Song* (Brooklyn, N.Y.: Hanging Loose Press, 2000), 13. Further references to this book are noted parenthetically in the text.

6. Quoted in Fraser, "Sherman Alexie's *Iowa Review* Interview."

7. Quoted in Fraser, "Sherman Alexie's *Iowa Review* Interview."

Chapter 7—*The Toughest Indian in the World*

1. Quoted in Cline, "About Sherman Alexie," 200.

2. Chapel, "Interview with Sherman Alexie."

3. Sybil Steinberg, review of *The Toughest Indian in the World, Publishers Weekly* 247, no. 16 (April 17, 2000): 52.

4. Seaman, "Read-alikes," 797.

5. Joanna Scott, "American Revolutions," *New York Times Book Review* 105, no. 21 (May 21, 2000): 14.

6. Scott, "American Revolutions," 15.

7. Scott, "American Revolutions," 15.

8. Sherman Alexie, *The Toughest Indian in the World* (New York: Atlantic Monthly Press, 2000), 29. Further references to this book are noted parenthetically in the text.

9. Quoted in Pabst, "Alexie Sends Strong Signals."

10. Quoted in Pabst, "Alexie Sends Strong Signals."

Chapter 8—*Ten Little Indians*

1. Sherman Alexie, *Ten Little Indians* (New York: Grove Press, 2003), 5. Further references to this book are noted parenthetically in the text.

Bibliography

Works by Sherman Alexie

Books

The Business of Fancydancing. Brooklyn, N.Y.: Hanging Loose Press, 1992.

Old Shirts and New Skins. Los Angeles: American Indian Studies Center, University of California, Los Angeles, 1993.

First Indian on the Moon. Brooklyn, N.Y.: Hanging Loose Press, 1993.

The Lone Ranger and Tonto Fistfight in Heaven. New York: Atlantic Monthly Press, 1993.

Reservation Blues. New York: Warner Books, 1995.

Indian Killer. New York: Warner Books, 1996.

The Summer of Black Widows. Brooklyn, N.Y.: Hanging Loose Press, 1996.

One Stick Song. Brooklyn, N.Y.: Hanging Loose Press, 2000.

The Toughest Indian in the World. New York: Atlantic Monthly Press, 2000.

Ten Little Indians. New York: Grove Press, 2003.

Articles

"Making Smoke." *Whole Earth* 94, no. 1 (Fall 1998): 102–3. Alexie's revealing account of making the feature film *Smoke Signals.*

"Death in Hollywood." *Ploughshares* 26, no. 4 (Winter 2000/2001): 7–10. An impassioned description of Alexie's disillusioning experiences in the business of mainstream filmmaking and his subsequent intentions to become an independent filmmaker.

Selected Works about Sherman Alexie

Web Sites

http://ShermanAlexie.com, hosted by www.fallsapart.com. Alexie's official Web site, with thorough and comprehensive information about speaking dates, book reviews, recordings, and essays.

Interviews

Campbell, Duncan. "Voices of the New Tribe." *Guardian* (Manchester), January 4, 2003. http://books.guardian.co.uk/review/story/0,12084,868123,00.html.

Chapel, Jessica. "Interview with Sherman Alexie." *Atlantic Monthly,* June 1, 2000. http://www.theatlantic.com/unbound/interviews/ba2000-06-01.htm.

Fraser, Joelle. "Sherman Alexie's *Iowa Review* Interview." http://www.english.uiuc.edu/maps/poets/a_f/alexie/fraser.htm. Originally published as "An Interview with Sherman Alexie," *Iowa Review* 30, no. 3 (Winter 2000): 59–70.

Highway, Tomson. "Spokane Words: Tomson Highway Raps with Sherman Alexie." *Aboriginal Voices,* January–March 1997. http://www.fallsapart.com/art-av.html.

Sidewalk. Interview with Sherman Alexie. 1999. http://www.falls apart.com/art-side.html.

Torrez, Juliette. "Juliette Torrez Goes Long Distance with Sherman Alexie." *Vice & Verse,* August 31, 1999. http://poetry.about.com/library/weekly/aa083199.htm?once=true&terms=alexia.

Selected Critical Analyses

Cline, Lynn. "About Sherman Alexie." *Ploughshares* 26, no. 4 (Winter 2000/2001): 197–202. Mostly biographical information about Alexie. Provides a helpful overview of his publications.

Cox, James. "Muting White Noise: The Subversion of Popular Culture Narratives of Conquest in Sherman Alexie's Fiction." *Studies in American Indian Literature* 9, no. 4 (Winter 1997): 52–70. An intriguing and compelling analysis of Alexie's work, mainly focusing on music in *Reservation Blues.*

Jorgensen, Karen. "White Shadows: The Use of Doppelgangers in Sherman Alexie's *Reservation Blues*." *Studies in American Indian Literature* 9, no. 4 (Winter 1997): 52–70. While topically narrow, Jorgensen's essay is a comprehensive and convincing analysis of doubles and mirroring in *Reservation Blues*.

Low, Denise. Review of *The Lone Ranger and Tonto Fistfight in Heaven*. *American Indian Quarterly* 20, no. 1 (Winter 1996): 123–26. While Low's contention that *The Lone Ranger and Tonto Fistfight in Heaven* is like a "casebook of postmodernist theory" is not substantially supported, her praising review does offer some intriguing ideas that place Alexie's work in the context of contemporary literary theory.

McFarland, Ron. "Sherman Alexie's Polemic Stories." *Studies in American Indian Literature* 9, no. 4 (Winter 1997): 27–38. McFarland's impressive analysis is extremely helpful in contextualizing Alexie's work within Native American history and culture.

McNally, Joel. "Sherman Alexie." *Writer* 114, no. 6 (June 2001): 28–31. A mostly biographical account of Alexie.

Pabst, Georgia. "Alexie Sends Strong Signals." *Milwaukee Journal Sentinel,* March 9, 2002. http://www.jsonline.com/enter/books/mar02/25632.asp. Part interview and part review of *The Toughest Indian in the World*.

Scott, Joanna. "American Revolutions." *New York Times Book Review* 105, no. 21 (May 21, 2000): 13–16. A review of *The Toughest Indian in the World*.

Seaman, Donna. "Read-alikes: Contemporary Native American Fiction." *Booklist* 97, no. 8 (December 15, 2000): 787–89. A review of *The Toughest Indian in the World*.

Skow, John. "Lost Heritage." *Time* 148, no. 19 (October 21, 1996): 88–90. A critical review of Alexie's *Indian Killer*.

Spencer, Russ. "What It Means to Be Sherman Alexie." *Book Magazine,* July/August 2000. http://www.bookmagazine.com/archive/issue11/alexie.shtml. Provides a comprehensive account of Alexie's career through 2000.

Steinberg, Sybil. Review of *The Toughest Indian in the World*. *Publishers Weekly* 247, no. 16 (April 17, 2000): 52.

Ullmann, Leslie. "Betrayals and Boundaries: A Question of Balance." *Kenyon Review* 15, no. 3 (Summer 1993): 182–96. An effusive review of Alexie's first published work, *The Business of Fancydancing*.

Index

Abdul-Jabbar, Kareem, 144
Adventures of Huckleberry Finn, The (Twain), 10–11
Alexie, Sherman: biography of, 1–6; *The Business of Fancy-dancing,* 3, 7, 15–29, 32, 34, 54, 61; *First Indian on the Moon,* 4, 40–56; *Indian Killer,* 4, 104–27, 138–39, 160; *I Would Steal Horses,* 3; *The Lone Ranger and Tonto Fist-fight in Heaven,* 4, 56–78; *Old Shirts and New Skins,* 29–39, 54; *One Stick Song,* 5, 142–51; *Reservation Blues,* 4, 78–104, 127, 151; *Smoke Signals,* 4–5, 7, 62; *The Summer of Black Widows,* 4, 127–42; *Ten Little Indians,* 5, 148, 173–91; *The Toughest Indian in the World,* 5, 148, 151–73
Ali, Mohammed, 144
anger, 15–16, 30, 38, 43, 47–48, 53, 57, 62, 65, 73, 75, 81, 104–5, 116–17, 125, 128, 142
Aschoff, Peter, 84
assimilation, 25
autobiography, 15, 41, 128, 142–43
awards, 4

baseball, 147
basketball, 26, 68, 73–75, 139–40, 143, 147, 168–69, 171, 188–91
Berryman, John, 15
Bevis, William, 8, 10–11
Bin Laden, Osama, 181
Black Elk Speaks, 114, 200n13
blues music, 81, 84, 86–92
Booklist, 142, 151
boxing, 152
Brady Bunch, The (television program), 66
Brando, Marlon, 51
Buffalo Bill, 28–29

camas root, 119
Catholicism, 13, 88, 99
celebrity, 50, 99
Checkers Records, 90
Chess Records, 90
Chief Joseph, 120
Christianity, 13, 88, 92, 96, 98–100
Citizen Kane (movie), 38
civil rights movement, 10
Cline, Patsy, 51, 154
colonialism, 9, 11, 36, 76, 86, 96
Columbus, Christopher, 36, 75
Coney Island, 141–42
confessional poetry, 15, 130
conservatism, 119
consumerism, 37
Cooper, James Fenimore, 10
cowboys, 48–49, 82, 160, 162

Cox, James, 56
coyote, 134–35
Crazy Horse, 16, 26–28, 34–35, 45, 75, 120
Custer, George Armstrong, 16, 27, 34–35, 129

Dachau, 140
Dean, James, 136
Deloria, Vine, Jr., 12, 135, 200n13
De Niro, Robert, 16, 51, 144
Dickinson, Emily, 39

Education of Little Tree, The (Carter), 114, 200n13
Ellensburg, Wash., 93
Ellison, Ralph, 84
environment, 12–13
Erdrich, Louise, 10
Ethiopia, 183
Eyre, Chris, 4

fancydancing, 16–17, 22, 187
Fargo, Donna, 144
Faulkner, William, 6, 78
feminism, 184
Fender, Freddy, 154
fire 41–43, 130–31
Flathead Indians, 152

Gaye, Marvin, 86
Generation X, 11
Geronimo, 120
Ghost Dance, 125–26

Godfather, The (movie), 38
Gonzaga University, 2
Great Gatsby, The (Fitzgerald), 10–11

Hanging Loose Press, 3
Hawthorne, Nathaniel, 10
Hayden, Robert, 33
Hendrix, Jimi, 6, 71, 86
Highway, Tomson, 78
history, 26
homophobia, 156
horses, 60, 86–87, 103
House Made of Dawn (Momaday), 10
humor, 2, 12, 15–16, 21, 71, 75–77, 108, 146, 180

identity, 7, 12, 24–25, 38, 54, 69–70, 73, 98, 120, 124, 133, 136, 148, 152, 164, 172–73, 176–77, 191
imagination, 18–20, 30, 38, 40–41, 43, 61–62, 75–76, 127–28, 134, 142, 158

Jesuits, 13, 88, 106, 110
Jews, 53
Johnson, Robert, 79, 85, 90, 93–94, 102–3
Jones, George, 154
Joplin, Janis, 79, 86, 136
Jorgensen, Karen, 85

Kafka, Franz, 61

Kennedy, John Fitzgerald, 25
Kincaid, James, 3
King, Thomas, 13
Kuo, Alex, 3

Lake-Thom, Bobby, 82
Lakota Woman (Crow Dog and
    Erdoes), 114, 200–201n13
Lame Deer: Seeker of Visions
    (Crow Dog and Erdoes), 114,
    200–201n13
Lee, Bruce, 50
Little Bighorn, 27
Lone Ranger, The, 56
Louis, Adrian C., 29
Low, Denise, 56
Lowell, Robert, 15

Macdonald, Andrew, 8, 13
magic realism, 16, 50, 79, 93
Mander, Jerry, 12
Manifest Destiny, 8, 24, 36, 49
Mexico, 172
Missoula, Mont., 93
Moby-Dick (Melville), 10–11
Mohawk tribe, 109
Momaday, N. Scott, 10–11
Monroe, Marilyn, 136
movies, 4–7, 38, 49–50
museums, 24, 29, 34

National Guard, 71
Native American: ceremonies, 19;
    community, 13, 21, 23, 38,
    54–55, 58, 63, 74, 82–83, 90,
102, 127, 140, 149; conception of time, 13; culture, 8,
11–13, 18, 22, 29, 37, 60–63,
80, 83, 87–88, 91, 98, 100,
105–6, 117, 121, 124, 134,
160, 174; drug and alcohol
abuse, 3, 9, 17, 21, 23, 26,
32–33, 41, 55, 58–59, 64, 75,
79, 81, 83, 101, 108, 187;
ecology, 9, 12–13; economy 9,
21, 32; education, 72–73; federal enrollment, 24, 31; history, 8–10, 62; HUD housing,
31, 54, 80; hybridization, 10,
116, 122, 166–67; languages,
8, 25; leaders, 60–61, 79, 99,
101; literature, 10–11, 14,
18–19, 30–31, 40, 114, 119,
132, 144; massacres, 8, 16,
35–37, 45, 96–97, 140–41;
music, 17, 84, 89, 98; powwows, 17, 23, 32, 111, 115,
148; purification ceremony,
137; relations with other
minorities, 53; religion, 12–13,
82, 84, 88, 98; reservations, 9,
11, 16, 19–23, 25, 30–31, 41,
43, 46, 51, 63, 68, 70 79–96,
98–99, 102, 107, 112, 125,
127, 145, 159, 168–70, 174;
rituals, 33; sacred sites, 46;
self-inflicted violence, 58–59,
72; songs, 18; traditions, 6, 10,
17, 22, 40, 44, 46, 59–60, 83,
87, 112, 188; tribes, 8, 10, 12,

Native American: tribes (*continued*),
18, 37, 100, 107, 110, 121,
134; visions, 60; warriors, 71,
79–80, 84, 90, 94, 101, 110,
116, 155, 191
Navajo Blues (movie), 4
Navajo tribe, 110
New Age movement, 9, 13–14,
88
New York, N.Y., 53, 93, 109
New York Times, 3, 152
Niatum, Diane, 18
nobel savage, 8, 10, 107, 132

owls, 113, 126

parody, 56
Phoenix, Ariz., 62
Plath, Sylvia, 15
popular culture, 6–7, 27, 37–38,
48, 50, 69, 80, 134, 162, 183
Portrait of a Lady, The (James),
10–11
Powwow Highway (movie), 4
Presley, Elvis, 79
Publishers Review, 151
Publishers Weekly, 131
punk music, 88, 91

racism, 58, 73, 119, 122, 144,
149, 177–78
Reardon, Wash., 2
rock music, 88, 91, 144
Rocky (movie), 50

Rowlandson, Mary, 10
Ruppert, James, 11

sarcasm, 15
Scott, Joanna, 152
Seaman, Donna, 142, 151
Seattle, Wash., 3, 5, 15, 64–66,
88, 119–20, 122–25, 176, 179
September 11, 2001, 5, 179,
181–82
sexuality, 137–38, 147–49,
151–52, 154–59, 161–66, 173,
179–80
Silko, Leslie Marmon, 10–11
Sioux tribe, 110
Sitting Bull, 35
Skow, John, 105
Slipstream Press, 4
Songs from This Earth on Turtle's Back (Bruchac), 3
Spokane, Wash., 3, 22, 25,
36–37, 53–54, 68, 103,
170–71
Spokane Indian Reservation, 1,
6, 15, 19, 135, 156, 175, 191
Spokane language, 2
Star Wars (movie), 50
Steinberg, Sybil, 151
stereotypes, 7, 60, 82, 88, 109,
169, 186
Streep, Meryl, 144
Sundance Film Festival, 5

Taos Poetry Circus World Heavyweight Championship, 5

television, 6–7, 11, 21, 27–28, 34, 37–38, 68–70, 82, 147
terrorism, 5, 180–81
Time magazine, 104–5
Tonto, 56
Trial, The (Kafka), 61
trickster, 11–12, 110, 133, 145
Twain, Mark, 10
Twitty, Conway, 154

Ullman, Leslie, 15
University of Washington, 111–12, 188

Velie, Alan, 74
Vietnam, 33
Vizenor, Gerald, 10–11

Walden Pond, 46
war, 5–6, 35, 71
Washington State University, 3, 172–73
Wayne, John, 49, 160–62
Weaver, Jace, 9, 12–13
Welch, James, 10–11
Western films, 34
Whitman, Walt, 139
Williams, Hank, 154
Wilson, Norma, 10
Woodstock, 72
World War II, 6, 146, 157
Wovoka, 120

Yakama tribe, 50